I0560685

QUAKE

Horror and Hope in Haiti

Will Loiseau

Quake: Horror and Hope in Haiti

Copyright © 2025 Will Loiseau

Second Edition

This is a work of nonfiction based on actual events. Some names and identifying details have been changed to protect the privacy of individuals.

All rights reserved. No part of this publication may be reproduced, distributed, or transmitted in any form or by any means, including photocopying, recording, or other electronic or mechanical methods, without the prior written permission of the publisher, except in the case of brief quotations embodied in critical reviews and certain other noncommercial uses permitted by copyright law.

Published by WL Media, a division of True Iron Will, LLC

1317 Edgewater Dr Suite 1297

Orlando FL 32804

ISBN: 979-8-9916451-3-3

IMAGE CREDITS

Author Photo: Conor Harrigan

Cover Photo: Damon Winter/The New York Times/Redux

Gallery Pages 9, 10: Joshua Trujillo/seattlepi.com

CONTENTS

DEDICATION

With love, I dedicate this book to my grandmother, the late Lucienne Martial. Her strength and calm demeanor remain an inspiration. Her spirit and influence will continue to live on way past her 103 years on this Earth. To my amazing parents, Wilfrid and Alberte, you've given me everything you could. Your faith in me is priceless. This book is also dedicated to the children and educators who lost their lives at College Catherine Flon and thousands of other schools across Haiti. To the late Prague Max Memnon, you were the embodiment of integrity.

PREFACE

The warm embrace and insightful feedback that greeted the first edition of *Quake* have been truly heartening. Your engagement, dear readers and thoughtful critics, has illuminated the path toward this revised and expanded second edition. It became clear that while the personal stories of the characters continue to form the heart of this narrative, there was an opportunity to enrich the reading experience further.

Many of you have expressed a keen interest in the intricate and often challenging history of Haiti, particularly the forces that have shaped its capital city and contributed to its vulnerabilities. In response, I've woven in additional historical context, hoping to offer a deeper understanding for those less familiar with Haiti's rich and complex past. It's a history that deserves to be known and appreciated.

Furthermore, given the subject matter, I've included a new section addressing the crucial matter of earthquake safety. It is my sincere hope that this practical information will be of value should any reader ever find themselves in such a precarious situation.

"The soil is, as a matter of fact, full of living organisms. It is essential to conceive of it as something pulsating with life, not as a dead or inert mass. There could be no greater misconception than to regard the earth as dead; a handful of soil is teeming with life."

- The Soil and Health: A Study of Organic Agriculture (Culture of the Land) by Sir Albert Howard

DÉJÀ VU

Powerful jolts trekked from hypocenter to epicenter. Tectonic motion of enormous underlying plates along the Enriquillo-Plantain Garden fault, crashed below the surface. Seismic, driving forces shifted the position of land masses forever. The earth had something to say. Its pulsating energy and stubborn grip held the world's full attention. Still, there was a glimmer of light and hope. The most horrifying threat is one that catches you when you least expect it.

January 10, 2010. A massive blanket of overcast sky covered south Florida that Sunday afternoon. The next day, Jean Carmelo and his parents were scheduled to board an early morning flight leaving Fort Lauderdale. The air was unusually crisp and unseasonably cold. Erratic weather patterns throughout the nation had left many on edge. Not far away, between the Caribbean Sea and the North Atlantic Ocean, an extreme system of a different kind had been in transit for quite some time.

Jean Carmelo was helping his mother pack her large suitcase with some last-minute items. They stood by the foot of the wooden bed with the suitcase laid open next to a travel bag. Something was not right. He had never seen her so annoyed. She told him that her left eyelid had been twitching.

Removing her glasses and closing her eyes, she aggressively tapped her eyelid. "This is what I don't like... This eye is getting on my last nerves!"

Jean Carmelo wanted to dismiss the chances of any real danger. She did have a tendency to worry about things she had no control over. Maybe the twitch was a symptom of the arthritis that had plagued her joints for years. It could have been some vitamin deficiency rather than a warning of something to come. But whatever was trying to communicate with her was also telling him that something was wrong. He had what felt like a gradually rising pit at the bottom of his stomach, and he had a tough time swallowing the gut feeling motoring up his throat. Rose appeared to be experiencing clarity about something.

* * * *

Four days earlier, a few minutes before seven a.m., Jean Carmelo's cell phone had rung. He was in front of his computer and studio recording gear, composing instrumental music—one of his hobbies. His mother's cell phone number flashed on the caller ID. He already knew why she was calling. The human connection was a fascinating phenomenon. One he had taken for granted on many occasions. They talked on the phone frequently, but he had a feeling that their conversation would be different that time around. He stopped the music.

Taking a deep breath, he picked up his phone. "Hello, Ma."

"How are you doing?" Rose sounded somewhat anxious, but she had an even tone.

"I'm fine. What's on your mind?"

Her variable breathing spoke volumes. She composed herself before saying, "I have some bad news. Grandma... my mother passed at three a.m."

"I'm sorry, Ma."

"She went away while she was sleeping."

Rose had gone to Port-au-Prince to see her mother no more than two weeks earlier. Jean Carmelo had encouraged her to go and was glad she did. He knew she wanted to be there to support her mother in the twilight of an illustrious journey. Now his mom would need him to support her. Jean Carmelo told her that he was happy she had followed her instincts to spend quality time with her mother. Their conversation turned to travel plans and funeral arrangements.

"Do you want to go?" Rose asked.

"I have to go. I'll notify my job."

"I will have to stay down there."

"For how long?" Jean Carmelo asked.

"I have to look at my calendar. At least fourteen days. How many days will your work let you take off?"

"Several. I have some bereavement days available to me too."

"I want to take the earliest plane this weekend," Rose said.

"I'll fly down to meet you in Florida, and then we can get on the same plane to Port-au-Prince."

"We have to hurry! You can buy your ticket to come here with the Internet?"

"Yes, I'll check the online fares," he said.

"I will make the reservations for us. I have the number somewhere for the travel agency. It's in my address book. I have to look."

"I'll get a one-way from Haiti back to New York... Is dad going too?"

"I don't know," she said. "He said he wants to go. I can't let him stay in the house by himself for two weeks. There's no one to stay with him. If you're not around to help me, it won't be easy traveling with him. The damage to his left-brain is affecting his right leg, and he refuses to use his right hand."

"I know Augustin would want to come with us too."

"With his job, it will be hard on such short notice."

"I'll call you back in a couple of hours, Ma."

"Love you."

"I love you too."

Jean Carmelo hadn't seen his grandmother in over a dozen years. He remembered the last time they'd embraced. Physically, she had been remarkably strong for someone so slender. Her spirit had been a key source of inspiration for him whenever he thought things weren't going so well in his life.

On a few occasions after his college graduation, he'd contemplated going to see her, but the cruel realities of political unrest held him back. When he closed his eyes at night, he dreamed of ruthless kidnappers demanding ransoms. When he woke up, the news supported his fears with gruesome true-to-life stories.

Armed street gangs had begun uprising against the Haitian government. Foreigners and Haitians were victim to broad daylight kidnappings and murders in Port-au-Prince. Kidnappers routinely fetched thousands of dollars in ransoms for American citizens. Many foreigners exercised diplomacy by avoiding the police and bargaining with gang members for their release. Despite the presence of police officers and armed multi-national U.N. guards, the abductions continued.

Jean Carmelo didn't want to put his family or himself in danger. He became discouraged and ultimately decided not to travel. Although he was disappointed that he would never again see his grandmother alive, he was glad that whatever pain or stress she'd been going through had been appeased.

Since his regular gym was closed for maintenance, Jean Carmelo had signed up for a temporary pass at a local gym. Channeling his energy would help him release anxiety. He felt as though he had to train and get ready for something, but he wasn't sure what. He had been performing high-intensity calisthenics, running, and weight training every day for the past couple of months.

The mixed martial arts and life philosophy he'd retained from Sifu Rey's school served as the perfect way to keep his training functional. Stress promotes rigid thoughts in the mind and stiff movements in the body. He'd learned the importance of improving his fluidity through smooth, flowing body expressions and deep breathing. That made co-existing with the spontaneous nature of life much easier. Continuous preparation became his sole motivation. Today, he lifted his body weight of 195 lbs. on the incline bench ten times. Last month, he'd struggled to hit five reps. An unyielding sense of urgency allowed him to quickly recover from his previous workouts, and he continued to make noticeable strength gains.

Grade school had taught him about the different classifications of food, but he'd never been clear on what he should or shouldn't eat. Every year brought some new diet plan claiming to take its followers to the pinnacle of health. He devoured online nutrition data and read books recommended by friends as a pastime. By eating more blueberries with oatmeal during breakfast and broccoli with chicken during dinner and occasionally fasting, he noticed a difference in his energy levels. Fish, eggs, yogurt, and beans kept him satiated most days. He continued to experiment toward being nutritionally sound and becoming more efficient.

HURDLES ON A TRIP

After explaining his situation to his supervisors at the bank, Jean Carmelo was consumed with anxiety. He was curious to see how much had changed in Port-au-Prince since his last visit. He wondered how the people were coexisting with the government. Who would he see there? What could he bring to give to those in need?

The night before his trip, he did some Internet research to get an idea of what the weather would be like before he packed. Haiti was expecting ninety degrees or better for the next several days. Name-brand clothing was as popular there as in the States, so he decided to pack light and only bring generic clothes to avoid unnecessary attention. Undergarments, basic T-shirts without logos, shorts, white sneakers, a navy blue suit with a white dress shirt, and navy shoes were all he would need.

The last day of the work week arrived in a flash. He got permission to leave work a little early, and he got home just in time to catch a cab to the Ronkonkoma train station for a 4:50 train. In the drop-off section, Jean Carmelo got out of the cab, retrieved his two black bags, and headed straight toward the ticket vending machine. He entered his request for a one-way ticket to Jamaica station.

After securing his ticket, receipt, and change, he walked toward the nearby pizzeria. Approaching the counter, he glanced through the glass at some cheese pies and ordered a slice. He wasn't hungry, but the peanuts or whatever thumbtack-sized snacks the airline would give out prompted his decision. They usually didn't cut it for a three-hour flight.

After getting his pizza, he jogged up the steps to where the train was waiting with open doors. Once in the car, Jean Carmelo placed the heavier of his bags on the metal rack directly above his seat. He sat down, relieved and in disbelief that he'd made it with time to spare. As the train began to move, a static voice announced where the train was headed.

Staring out the car window and eating his slice of pizza, Jean Carmelo saw the reflection of a group of young girls who could've been fresh out of high school or just starting college. They were chatting, smacking on chewing gum, and searching their pocketbooks for lip gloss and compact mirrors. They huddled over their mobile phones, sharing pictures and text messages that made them giggle.

Then Jean Carmelo remembered that he had not brought along his camera charger. He didn't think he'd take more than a few dozen pictures though. It'd been weeks since he used the camera last, and he figured that charging it the night before would be enough for it to last the entire trip.

He hadn't slept well and decided to shut his eyes for a short while. He set the alarm on his phone to wake him up in fifteen minutes. For some reason, he'd never felt comfortable sleeping on trains. Maybe it was an adverse effect from all of the Charles Bronson movies he grew up watching with his dad. *What if I oversleep? I'll wake up wishing I was still dreaming.*

He felt a vibration. Slowly opening his eyes, he was stunned that fifteen minutes had already elapsed. He didn't even remember falling asleep. A muffled voice announced over the PA system that Jamaica station was the next stop. Jean Carmelo's plan was to get on the next available Air Train to John F. Kennedy International Airport in order to be at the gate forty-five minutes before his 6:10 PM flight. Any misstep would be disastrous. JetBlue had a strict policy about check-ins. The train slowly came to a complete stop.

When the sliding doors opened, he asked a conductor on the platform, "What's the quickest way to the Air Train?"

"You go up that flight of steps and make a right when you get to the top. You'll see the arrows directing you to the terminals," the conductor said, pointing toward his left.

"Thanks." With a bag in each hand, Jean Carmelo darted up the long flight of concrete and metal steps.

He proceeded to get a five-dollar MetroCard from the touch-screen machine without any trouble. Trains came every ten minutes, and within five, the next one pulled in. Two dozen passengers stepped in once the doors opened.

The train was open with rows of yellow and orange bench seats along the edges. When the train left the terminal, Jean Carmelo got an attractive view of the airport. The car was clean, and the ride was smooth. As soon as the train came to his stop, he darted into the terminal and jogged through a tunnel to the security check point just around the corner.

Although he had been hearing about a lengthy list of proposed security changes, Jean Carmelo didn't notice anything different about the personnel or the procedures that passengers had to go through before collecting their belongings on the other side of the X-ray machines. He readjusted his belt, put his sneakers back on, and retrieved his bags. Everything seemed to be business as usual as he walked through the airport. He got to the gate a few minutes before an announcement was made that it was time for passengers going to Fort Lauderdale to form a line to begin boarding.

To Jean Carmelo, aeronautics was without exception, one of man's most amazing feats. He often marveled over how people were able to be in a country one minute and arrive in a foreign land thousands of miles away hours later. Once he boarded, he sat in his seat and looked out the window. He knew right away from the darkening sky that he wasn't going to stay awake for the duration of the flight.

Hours later, Jean Carmelo woke up suddenly from a dream in which he was freefalling from a light blue sky. A few napkins and a small bag of chips were lying on the tray table in front of him. The increase in cabin pressure had him searching his pants pockets for gum. Fasten seat belt lights came on over each seat as the plane began to make its descent. His mp3 player had been off the entire flight but in the back of his mind he wondered if turning it on would really interfere with the pilots' communication with tower control. *Could a cell phone disrupt the pilots' panel intstruments?* He was always skeptic about whether or not these small portable devices could actually cause an aircraft to lose power.

Using the intercom, the stewardess reminded everyone to remain in their seats with seatbelts fastened until the lights above went off and the plane reached the gate. Shortly after, the plane touched down. Before the fasten seatbelt lights went off the race to hurry up and wait began. Dozens of passengers who suffered from "not able to remain seated" tried to squeeze themselves into the lone center aisle. Simultaneously, they attempted to retrieve their bags from the overhead bins.

Jean Carmelo took some time to sort things out in his mind. *Mentally, I've got to be tough enough to handle seeing Grandma in an altered state. How will she look? This trip is going to be something else. Physically, traveling with mom and dad is gonna be tough. They might end up looking to me for support and direction. Spiritually, something tells me I will be tested. I haven't been there in so long. I'm gonna stick out. I'm not fluent in the language. The way I've been living over here and the way the people over there have been living, it's like two alternate universes.*

It would be crucial for him to expect the unexpected.

SUNSHINE BLUES

As he walked through the Fort Lauderdale-Hollywood International Airport, Jean Carmelo noticed tall palm trees swaying on the other side of the thick windows. He headed outside. The humid heat smacked him right across his face. He walked over to a dark-skinned man standing by a booth with a round black-and-white checkered logo. The man asked him if he needed a cab. Jean Carmelo nodded and told him he was going to Tamarac.

The man motioned to one of his co-workers, who drove up to the curb in a white cab. The driver opened the trunk, and Jean Carmelo shoved his bags in and got inside the car. Calming himself, he looked around as they drove off.

"Where are you going?" the driver asked.

"I'm going to 3624 Spring Drive, right off of University," Jean Carmelo said.

He partook in some small talk with the cab driver, originally from Russia, who said he'd lived in New York as well. They turned off of the main road onto the wide streets of his parents' retirement neighborhood. The area looked familiar, especially because Jean Carmelo had been there numerous times. No matter how many times he had visited, it was difficult to navigate directly to the address. Each neat suburban house appeared the same. Even more so now that it was dark outside. Community laws dictated that all houses be painted white. Every house was practically the same size, and their front and backyards had barely any variations.

After the cab pulled up at his parents' house, Jean Carmelo stepped out and retrieved his bags from the trunk. When his mom opened the door, he smiled and bent down to embrace her.

"How are you, Ma?"

"I'm so happy to see you, son," she said, gently rubbing his bald head.

As they hugged, he looked over her shoulder and caught his father's eye. Jules, wearing a white collared shirt, was sitting at the far end of the table with a happy, blank expression. It was the same look he'd had a year ago when Jean Carmelo came to visit after his father's stroke. Although Jules was physically able to stand up by using a cane and could stride slowly without one, he remained seated. Clearly his dad had not made much progress.

Jean Carmelo walked over to him and extended his right hand. Jules labored to lift his arm, indicating some slight discomfort. They shook hands, and hugged. Jean Carmelo couldn't help but think about their almost-daily telephone conversations. His encouragement hadn't done much of anything to motivate his father to improve his condition. He wanted his father to understand that the determining factor in recovery would come from his effort.

"How have you been?" Jean Carmelo asked.

"So far, so good," Jules replied.

"How was your flight?" Rose asked.

"Both airports were packed! There wasn't an empty seat on board. Not much turbulence in the air though, and the landing was cool," Jean Carmelo said. As fatigued as he was, he didn't want to show it.

Rose stood across from him on the other side of the stainless steel kitchen sink. "How are you? Did you get taller?"

"No, Ma, no one grows taller after thirty." He laughed.

"Are you sure? Well, it's good to have you here with us."

"I love that we're all here together right now," he said.

"You look like you've been exercising a lot."

"Yes, some days I don't feel like doing anything, but I always feel much better once I get started," Jean Carmelo said.

He wanted to avoid sounding like a late night infomercial, but he also wanted to subtly nudge Jules, who had yet to move from his chair. Jean Carmelo noticed that his father didn't seem interested in joining their discussion. Jules's ability to remember just about anything had declined tremendously in the last few years. He was demonstrating the preliminary stages of Alzheimer's disease. Combined with his deep-rooted reluctance to engage in physical activities, his chances for a full recovery were slim.

The next morning Jean Carmelo got up before the sun rose. In his boxer shorts and white T-shirt, he walked to the kitchen to grab a cup of cold, filtered water from the refrigerator. After nursing the cup for a half hour or so, he began his push-ups. The routine was his way of increasing his blood flow and proving to a higher power that he deserved to see another day.

Soon after, Rose made her way into the kitchen. "You see? I knew I heard the sound of Bigfoot."

"Good morning, Mom." Jean Carmelo smiled.

"Before you came last night, I tried printing the tickets for the plane. I don't think the printer is good. Do you know how to fix it?"

"Sure, I can look at it. But the only things we'll need are our passports and driver's licenses... unless we're able to print boarding passes."

"I don't know, maybe the ink is finished," she said. "If you have time, there's the drug store on University. You know the one. They can refill it."

Minutes later, Jules got out of bed, allowing muscle memory to direct him to the dining room chair. He wore a distant expression with a half a smile. He waited to be fed breakfast or for someone to bring him the newspaper. Jean Carmelo was on the computer, troubleshooting issues with the printer. Rose sat on a stool with her medical supplies spread out on the counter. She squeezed a drop of blood from her finger onto a test strip before placing it in a meter. A beep came from the small machine.

Jean Carmelo looked over at her. "Are you all right over there?"

"This morning it reads 130," she said, her face uncertain.

"Was it that high yesterday?" he asked.

"No. I don't remember eating anything that would raise it so high."

"We'll keep an eye on what you're eating today and see if we can figure something out."

"Yes, doctor," she joked.

Thick weeds of inactivity continued to grow underneath Jules's feet as he sat still and stared into space. Jean Carmelo knew that his father's current routine was counter-productive to progress, and he wanted to do what he could to help his father change for the better, at least for while he was there.

He walked over to Jules. "Good morning, Dad!"

"Good morning, my son," he replied with a smile.

"How did you sleep last night?"

"Very well, no problems."

"Sometime this morning, I'm going to go for a walk. Would you like to join me?" Jean Carmelo rubbed his hands together.

"No, I go walking every day. I have no choice." Jules replied.

Jean Carmelo knew his father's idea of "walking" was taking a dozen or so steps to the next available chair. He made a concerted effort to watch his father's physical movements and listen to his speech patterns.

When Jules didn't see the newspaper on the dining room table where Rose usually put it, he asked Jean Carmelo where it was. The night before, Jean Carmelo had asked Rose to move the paper while he was there because Jules would make a minimal effort to search for it if it wasn't in the same place each morning. Jean Carmelo suggested that they go together to search for the newspaper.

"I paid money for the paper, and I don't see it!" Jules snapped, adjusting his glasses.

Jean Carmelo was pleased to catch a glimpse of the man he'd known while growing up. He had a purpose and seemed determined. Jean Carmelo calmly replied, "I know. That's why I want to help you find it now."

Pretending not to hear them, Rose stood in the kitchen, emptying the dishwasher. She knew that Jean Carmelo had put the newspaper on the leather sofa in the Florida room. Jean Carmelo watched his father use the cane to help himself up off the chair. The right side of his body had been severely affected by the stroke, and he had only regained partial movement. When he was up, Jean Carmelo instructed Jules to leave his cane there.

Jules barked, "What do you want me to do, fall?"

For the past three years, he had been arguing with medical personnel and anyone else who would listen, telling them he couldn't do things. He would say it with such conviction that if one didn't know any better, they would believe him. In actuality, he was able to walk without a cane as long as he kept his head up and wasn't distracted or attempting to walk too fast.

"I'm right here, and I won't let you fall," Jean Carmelo reassured.

Jules looked Jean Carmelo in the eye and put his cane to the side. They proceeded to move from the dining room with Jean Carmelo standing in front, facing him. Jean Carmelo used hand gestures to remind Jules to keep his head facing forward and shoulders back. Jules kept his hands by his sides, clenched tight.

"Open up your hands," Jean Carmelo calmly instructed, trying not to derail his progress with negative thoughts. "Keep them open in order to grab hold of something if you lose your balance."

Jules could move his left foot easily, but he labored to drag the right foot along. Jean Carmelo could practically see Jules's brain working to absorb information while adjusting to the change in scenery. Jules obviously hadn't done that much walking in weeks, and he became increasingly frustrated with each stride. In the Florida room, a large mirror decorated the wall next to them.

"Take a break if you like. Look into the mirror so you can see your posture," Jean Carmelo said.

Jules looked at his reflection, raising his eyebrows for a second as if he surprised by what he saw. The look of determination in his eyes got Jean Carmelo excited. Jules was attempting to accomplish a goal. He was exercising. Then Jules's attention focused on something he spotted while glancing in the mirror. On the sofa behind him was the yellow plastic bag that contained the newspaper.

"It's over there. I pay money for that!" Jules said.

"That's right! You had to find it."

As Jules readied himself to sit on the sofa, Jean Carmelo caught a glimpse of the gears moving in his father's brain. *How should I position myself to sit? Where should I put these two sofa pillows? Should I hold the paper or place it down on the armrest? What about my cane?* Those were all questions he knew his father was asking himself.

They'd had a small success, but it would be quite some time before Jules got up again. That was a problem Jean Carmelo didn't have the solution for yet. On some days, Jules would acknowledge his own lack of effort, but that recognition wouldn't prevent him from continuing to sit indefinitely. Jean Carmelo was curious to see how long it would take before Jules would attempt to get up on his own.

"I'll be in the bedroom making some phone calls. You can call me if you need me," Jean Carmelo said.

"Okay," Jules answered, relieved to rest.

After an hour of working on the PC and another hour napping in the back bedroom, Jean Carmelo woke up and found Jules right where he'd left him. When Jean Carmelo initiated conversation about what Jules had read in the newspaper, he got minimal feedback. Jules answered every question with incomplete phrases or "I don't remember."

Later that day, Rose called the pick-up service to confirm their ride to their airport the next day.

Since he had to get back to work, Jean Carmelo would only spend a week in Haiti, but his mom and dad would stay for two weeks. Jules hadn't traveled outside the country in years, and he seemed to have no interest in packing his bags. When Jean Carmelo asked him what he wanted to pack, Jules looked at him blankly.

"Did you hear what I asked you?" Jean Carmelo asked.

"Just give me some shirts and shorts," Jules responded.

Jean Carmelo reminded him that he would also need socks, shoes, and undergarments.

Jules said, "Yeah, whatever you think is good."

Jean Carmelo brought his dad into the master bedroom, and Jean Carmelo dug through his father's shirts in the bedroom closet. Many of them still bore price tags or were covered in the thin, clear plastic from the dry cleaners. Jean Carmelo had always admired his father's taste in shirts. The four large pockets and pleats down the front or the back gave off a regal appeal that complemented his demeanor. Jules once told him that these shirts got their origin during the early 1700's when immigrant farmers in the Caribbean fields would fill as many pockets as they could with guava fruit. This was one of many historical facts he once freely dictated that had now disappeared from his memory like forgotten socks in a dryer.

Ever since his mild stroke, he hadn't cared much about his appearance. A week earlier, after days of pleading, Rose had finally convinced him to have his hair, beard, and nails trimmed by a local barber. Jean Carmelo had noticed that any activity involving decision-making made his father lose patience and he avoided them as much as possible.

"Is this tan shirt okay?" Jean Carmelo asked, knowing that the answer for anything he held up would be affirmative.

"Yeah, that's good," was his predictable reply.

While Jean Carmelo packed his father's clothes, Jules slowly began to show more interest. He even asked for certain items of clothing he remembered wearing weeks or months earlier. By midnight, the last of his parents' bags had been packed with two weeks' worth of clothes.

FLA TO PAP

Ten minutes later than the time they were all scheduled to meet, the taxi arrived out front. Jean Carmelo greeted the driver when he knocked at the door and helped him carry the luggage out to the car. A strong gust of wind whipped through the empty streets. Jean Carmelo couldn't remember it ever being so cold down there. In less than twenty-four hours, the temperature had dropped more than thirty degrees.

Using his cane, Jules walked to the front door with a limp. He lifted his stronger leg up and over the elevated door sill plate before dragging the weaker leg over. He immediately complained that it was windy and cold. The frigid breeze became aggressive and pierced through their light jackets and sweaters.

When they drove off, Rose and Jules noticed that Jean Carmelo had put the trash can at the edge of the driveway for pick up the next day. For old time's sake, an argument ensued. His parents thought that leaving the empty can in front of the house for the next two weeks would scream that the house was unattended.

When they got to the airport, Jean Carmelo found a wheelchair for his father, and they checked their luggage at the podium with the American Airlines logo.

"How many bags are you checking?" the ticket agent asked, looking at the bags in Jean Carmelo's hands.

"I don't want to check any. Is this one too big to carry on?" Jean Carmelo asked. "On my flight here, I carried on both of these bags."

"That must not have been this airline sir. Our policy requires an additional payment fee to carry on more than one bag."

"Okay, I'll check this one in," Jean Carmelo said reluctantly.

The agent took the bag and printed out their boarding passes and baggage claim tickets. She handed them to Jean Carmelo. "Go up to the elevator and proceed to gate F5. Enjoy your flight."

"Thanks," he said. With all three passports in his hands, it hit him that those booklets were their most valuable material possessions.

At the TSA checkpoint, a middle-aged woman wearing a navy blue TSA uniform told Jean Carmelo that if his dad could walk, they would assist him through the detector. Her badge said her name was Monique.

On cue, Jules began his cantankerous display. "It's cold in here!"

Maintaining his composure, Jean Carmelo suggested that Jules follow her instructions. The last thing Jean Carmelo wanted was for security to prevent them from getting on their flight. He guided his father's wheelchair to the gray scanner and grabbed his hand to help him up. Jules clutched his arm as they inched forward until TSA personnel told him that Jean Carmelo couldn't walk through with his father. Monique, who was waiting on the other side of the scanner, took Jules's hands and helped him back into his chair once he was on the other side.

Jean Carmelo emptied the last of what was in his pant pockets and walked through the scanner with Rose not far behind him. The whole experience felt as though it had lasted way longer than it needed to. Over to their left were the men's and women's restrooms, and they all had to go.

Rose went off to use the women's room, and Jean Carmelo and Jules went off to the men's. Then it struck Jean Carmelo that Jules would need help. He was fine at home when he could take as much time as he wanted, but how would he function when he was on a clock?

Jean Carmelo could move more quickly than Jules, so he went first as soon as a urinal became available. Jules stepped up next, using his cane. As awkward a moment as it was, it wasn't as complicated as Jean Carmelo thought it would be. He could only imagine what his dad had done for him when he was a young kid.

Once they were done, they walked over to the sink to wash and dry their hands. Jules sat back down in the chair, and Jean Carmelo wheeled him off. When they made their way out, Rose stood in front of an ATM and waited for them. That was how Jean Carmelo knew they had taken a long time inside.

They finally got to the departure gate with at least fifteen minutes to spare. Sitting down across from a large window in the boarding area, they stared at two flat screen televisions. One displayed up-to-the-minute flight departure and arrival times, and the other had on local and world news.

Jean Carmelo leaned toward his mother. "I never asked you about the funeral arrangements."

"A limousine is supposed to pick us up from Grandma's house and take us to the viewing that starts at eight a.m. After that, the funeral will be from ten to eleven a.m."

Jean Carmelo tried to picture in his mind what it would be like to ride around in a limo in Port-au-Prince. He couldn't envision a clear scene that made sense. He trusted his mom knew what she was doing and left it at that. He wanted to ask her how much of the funeral costs was coming out of her pocket, but he also knew that whatever the price was, she would happily pay it to see her mom placed to rest respectfully.

"What day will the viewing be?" he asked.

"The only days the funeral parlor had available were Tuesday and Thursday. I chose Thursday."

Jean Carmelo studied the boarding passes he was holding. He noticed that they would not be seated in the same area of the plane. His parents were seated next to each other at the front of the plane, and his seat number was thirty-five. He didn't mind at all.

A few minutes behind schedule, a silver Boeing 737 approached. As the plane pulled in, passengers grabbed their belongings. Most were familiar with the drill, forming lines before the gate agent could make the announcement.

Twenty minutes later, after the passengers had settled in, the flight crew was prepared for takeoff. Jean Carmelo looked around and was surprised that the majority of the passengers were Caucasian. Most of them were in their mid-twenties, thirties, and forties. They wore light blue T-shirts identifying themselves as members of the same group. Many foreigners valued Haiti as a vacation spot, especially at that time of year. The weather was warm, the beaches were beautiful, and the cost of living was cheap.

Haiti was divided into the haves and the have-nots. This was the reality ever since French colonists enforced slavery during the 1700's. The white elite owned black slaves, which enabled them to take advantage with an economic and social leverage. Even after the Haitian revolution in the late 1700's diminished the colonial ruling class, the wealthy class re-emerged. They were mostly French-speaking mulattoes who inherited their freedom and other privileges. In contrast, those who did not have access to food, clean water, employment and other basic necessities were dark-skinned. Historically, the racism amongst Haitians marked a preference for lighter complexions.

Jean Carmelo spent most of the flight sleeping, but he woke up in time to hear the pilot announce that the aircraft was flying on-time and would be making its descent shortly. Jean Carmelo felt goose bumps rise on his arms. He focused his attention out the window at the striking contrast between Haiti and the Dominican Republic. Before being colonized by Europeans, the island was inhabited by Taino Indians who named it "Ayiti", which means "mountainous country" or "land of mountains." The calcareous characteristics of the mountains were a sight to see, but the recent hurricane seasons had been unforgiving. Due to extreme soil erosion, the country's land was headed toward desertification.

Many of the trees had either been swept away by storms or cut down to make charcoal or sell in the market places. The plush, green forests, farmland, and wealth of vegetation on the Dominican side, compared to the rocky and more nutritionally void landscape of Haiti, were heartbreaking. Years ago, Jules had told Jean Carmelo that at one time, this was where most of the world's coffee was produced. It was clear that Haitian life as they once knew it was in serious danger.

As everyone fastened their seat belts, put up their tray tables, and returned their seats to the upright position to prepare for landing, Jean Carmelo imagined what the next several days would be like. Their touchdown on the tarmac was a bit rough, but he, along with the rest of the passengers, showed their appreciation for a safe landing by giving the pilot and crew a round of applause.

HOT AND STICKY

They had arrived at Toussaint L'ouverture International Airport in Port-au-Prince, named after the charismatic governor-general who helped lead Haiti's revolt against France. Near the end of his life, as he faced betrayal and capture, Toussaint had declared, "By overthrowing me, you have only defeated the trunk of the tree of freedom; it will grow back because its roots are deep, numerous, and vivacious." His words proved prophetic - Haiti would indeed gain its independence after his death. Now, centuries later, the airport bearing his name stood as a gateway to the nation he helped birth.

As they taxied toward the gate, Jean Carmelo was struck by the emptiness of the tarmac - where he was used to seeing dozens of planes and bustling ground crews in New York, here there were only scattered ground vehicles and workers moving at an unhurried pace. Their plane might have been the only one arriving at that moment.

The warm, humid air began to gradually seep into the aircraft cabin, replacing the artificial chill of recycling air conditioning. Jean Carmelo felt his clothes slowly beginning to cling to his skin, though not enough to restrict his movement. Through the large but visibly aged windows of the plain terminal building, he could see the worn brown tiles that would soon be under their feet - so different from the carpeted corridors of JFK or LaGuardia.

That familiar, mineral smell of sun-baked building materials wafted through the cabin - an unmistakable scent that whispered "Port-au-Prince" to some deep part of his memory. Though others might have found it strange or unpleasant, to Jean Carmelo it carried a sense of welcome, of return.

He tried to scan the front of the plane where his mom and dad were sitting but couldn't see them through the sea of increasingly restless passengers. The nervous energy in the cabin was palpable as people began shifting in their seats, half-standing despite the still-illuminated seatbelt sign, reaching anxiously for bags in the overhead compartments. Their movements had a protective quality - hands clutching carry-ons close to their bodies, eyes darting to track their belongings. They all knew what awaited them at baggage claim: a chaotic scramble where bags could easily disappear into the wrong hands.

As soon as the seatbelt light went off, this simmering tension erupted into action. Men, women and children jumped up as one, a silent but fierce competition to be first off the plane, first to the carousel, first to secure their possessions. The cramped aisle filled instantly with bodies and bags, everyone trying to squeeze past each other toward the exit.

As Jean Carmelo moved to the aisle to remove his bags from the overhead compartment, he felt bags brushing against his lower leg. The line exiting the plane moved at a slow pace. He wondered why he was continuously being pushed. He turned to see who was holding those bags, and he looked into the eyes of a short Haitian woman who didn't seem to understand courtesy. He excused himself and moved on.

He walked through the airport halls with his carry-on bags, wondering how his parents had managed to move out of his sight so quickly. When he found them, they were in a crowded lobby amongst people who had just gotten off or were looking to board flights. A Haitian man was pushing Jules's wheelchair over to a counter where Rose was filling out paperwork.

Rose snapped at Jean Carmelo, "You didn't see us standing here? When are you going to stop being so selfish?"

He raised his eyebrows. "What did you want me to do? Jump over ten rows of people?"

Jean Carmelo calmed himself down. He lowered his voice in respect and as an example of leadership. It had been a long day with a tough landing. The chaos they'd faced in Fort Lauderdale would surely be minimal compared with the madness waiting for them there.

He asked one of two women behind the counter for the same paper his mom was filling out. Each person seeking to enter the country had to complete an entry form with questions written in French and Kreyol. He could fill out the lines requiring name, date of birth, place of birth, and reason for travel. For the questions he didn't understand, he asked his mom for a translation. Rose was a bit stressed. Jules's inability to write transferred those duties to her.

When they were done with their forms, they handed them to an employee sitting behind the counter. The woman snapped her gum and took a few seconds to enjoy her cell phone's loud, melodic ringtone before answering it. She talked casually while processing their passports. Jean Carmelo understood that Haiti didn't share the hustle of JFK, but he wondered if she truly valued her position as one of a miniscule number of Haitians with a paying job.

Rose and Jean Carmelo, pushing Jules in a wheelchair, walked out to the baggage claim area. Piles of bags were scattered near a large window with a wide view of the runway. The room buzzed with the chatter from the crowd inside. Airport workers wearing orange uniforms with name tags stood and talked and aided passengers. Bags of all shapes, sizes, and colors were stacked up everywhere. There was no carousel to go to.

Jean Carmelo left his parents in the middle of the spacious room and went searching for their bags. After a few moments of frustration from grabbing look-alikes, he picked out all five of their bags and brought them over to Jules and Rose. They were ready to go outside and find their ride.

"Do you have five singles to give to the nice man pushing your father?" Rose asked Jean Carmelo.

"I'll take care of him when we get outside." Jean Carmelo, pushing their luggage cart, told her.

The closer Jean Carmelo and his parents got to the exit doors, the more they heard and felt the energy of the people outside. They stepped outside and were met with bright, hot sunlight. Hundreds of Haitians with various agendas packed the front of the airport, their eyes honed in on new arrivals. Many others waited on the other side of a tall link fence in the distance. The older man who had helped Jean Carmelo and his family with their bags earlier proceeded to lead them to where their ride was waiting for them.

A rude and impatient middle-aged woman bumped Jean Carmelo's leg with her bags. He wondered if it was the same woman who'd hit him on the plane, but it was another impatient traveler to whom he paid no mind. Jean Carmelo looked over to his left and noticed that a man pushing a luggage cart was giving Rose's legs similar treatment. Jean Carmelo walked over to her and positioned himself behind his mom, giving the man a stare that invited him to try the same with him.

"Desolé!" The man apologized as if he had not been aware of what he was doing.

Jean Carmelo nodded, said nothing, and kept moving. A tall, skinny man in beige uniform approached Jean Carmelo out of nowhere. He placed his bony fingers on the handle of the luggage cart, offering to help.

Jean Carmelo had things under control, but he respected the man's gesture, so he stepped back and let him push the cart.

As soon as he let go of the cart, Jean Carmelo sensed that that move carried further implications. Jean Carmelo felt the crowd observing his mannerisms, attire, and bags. They were probably trying to determine whether or not he had gotten off a plane from the States or some other affluent country. When Jean Carmelo turned to his left, the man he'd let push the cart spoke to him softly in Kreyol.

"Mwen genyen twa ti moun lakay mwen, mwen pa genyen anyen pou-m ba yo manje. Tanpri, eske ou kapab ban-m senk dola ou sa ou kapab?" *I've been having trouble feeding my three kids at home. Please, sir, can you find kindness in your heart and give me five dollars or whatever you can?*

Good job, Jean Carmelo! He thought. *Not even thirty minutes in Port-au-Prince and people are already successfully running game on you.*

He heard a female call his mom's name. He lightly placed his hand on his mom's shoulder and pointed her toward the voice. A woman came from behind the fence to greet them and introduced herself as Leslie. Leslie, in a flowery sundress, was short with a kindly face, slightly crooked teeth, and bright brown eyes. She was accompanied by her friend, Jacques, who would drive them to their destination.

They all smiled and exchanged pleasantries before walking to Jacques' car. It looked too small to transport all five of them. It had four doors, but the thought of packing themselves in with all their bags made Jean Carmelo cringe. They had barely been able to make it happen with one less person and a much larger car in Florida!

The man next to Jean Carmelo shifted his level of despair into higher gear. Jean Carmelo felt obligated to help people while on his trip, so he handed the man a five-dollar bill. Rose saw the transaction and quickly ordered the man to give the money to the older man who had been helping them. He pretended not to hear her. He positioned himself behind Jean Carmelo to politely help pack bags into the car. That infuriated Rose and the older man.

He looked at them and pleaded his case. "Tanpri, ban m'..." *Please give me...*

Jean Carmelo thought, *Trying to be nice is not an effective way to help anyone.* In a flash, the tall man disappeared. Rose pulled out three singles to attempt to compensate the older man for Jean Carmelo's misjudgment. Jean Carmelo felt horrible.

The car was bursting at the seams with luggage, and no one was even in yet. The trunk was tiny and already had a spare tire in it. Getting everything inside without getting violent with the bags and the trunk lid didn't seem likely. Only three bags fit in the trunk, and the rest had to go in the car cabin. Rose, Leslie, and Jean Carmelo took ten minutes to squeeze into the back seat with the last of suitcases. Jules sat in the front passenger seat with the light carry-on bags resting on his lap. After slamming the door twice against his hip, Jean Carmelo's door shut. Jacques got in last to make sure all of the doors were shut properly.

It must have been at least ninety-degrees outside with barely a breeze, and all of the car windows were up. The only body part Jean Carmelo could move freely was his left arm, so he reached over to put down the window. Through the rearview mirror, Jacques noticed Jean Carmelo and said that he would put on the air conditioning. Jean Carmelo didn't think a car that beat up would have air conditioning, so he was relieved to know they wouldn't roast to death in a Toyota Corolla.

Jacques moved his seat forward to accommodate Jean Carmelo and asked, "Is everyone's door locked? Keep your windows up at all times!"

Although the air conditioning was on high, it barely kept beads of sweat from forming on their foreheads. The relentless sun reflected off of the grey concrete roads and penetrated the vehicle's interior. It didn't take long to understand Jacques' concerns.

As soon as the car joined the long line of cars headed toward the only exit, dozens of grown men and young kids tapped their hands and placed their faces against the windows. Pedestrians yelled curse words at drivers. Beggars in dusty, oversized T-shirts and shorts with holes and sweats stains wandered through the cars. They all looked inside and saw the bags as resources they did not have.

Jacques explained to everyone inside that they couldn't give them anything. He had made the trip often and had many a story to tell about robberies and carjackings. They were common throughout the country, especially in an area with such a high concentration of new visitors. New arrivals were notoriously sized up for later assaults and stick ups. Those who blindly gave handouts put themselves in danger of being hunted down.

One boy, no older than eight or nine years old, relentlessly pursued potential generosity. He ran alongside the car, looked into each of their eyes, and tapped on the windows, begging them to give him anything to survive. Jean Carmelo was hurt to see such a genuine plea and be unable to do anything. The boy moved from one side of the vehicle to the other, explaining that his parents had died and he was left to take care of his younger brother. They all stared straight ahead, trying to block out his cries. To give the boy even a penny could have easily resulted in a riot.

The Corolla, with its sputtering engine, singing shocks, and squeaky breaks, came up to a large mosh pit of cars, trucks, and motorcycles disguised as a traffic circle. If not for an iron-gate around the middle of the circle, most drivers would have driven through it. The hyper airport traffic abruptly dispersed into the early afternoon smog.

The car didn't have a radio, so conversation began. Jean Carmelo was cordial, but with his limited command of Kreyol, he remained respectfully quiet. He zoned out, looking at the mountains on both sides. Up on the hills were slum villages with hundreds of small shacks with sheet metal roofs and walls made from straw or brittle concrete. Those homes were built practically on top of each other. Haiti had no building codes. Many people lived as squatters. The destruction caused by 2008's hurricane season was as devastating up close as it was from the air.

Rows of clotheslines with colorful garments were hung outside most of the makeshift dwellings. Along the sidewalks and in the streets, thousands of Haitians moved with worker-ant frenzy. It all looked the same as when Jean Carmelo had been there more than twelve years earlier. He wasn't sure what exactly he'd expected, but he had wanted to see some signs of improvement. There were absolutely none.

There were no rules about driving on those streets either. Traffic was supposed to drive on the right side of the road, but there were no lane markings. Traffic lights and signs were non-existent. The weight of so many people in the car put a tremendous strain on the suspension. It squealed with the brakes anytime they stopped or went over one of the plentiful potholes. The manhole-sized craters were so deep that Jean Carmelo couldn't see the bottom from where he was sitting. Drivers made all kinds of unpredictable maneuvers to avoid them, almost causing a number of collisions.

They passed a Texaco station. It looked exactly as it had when Jean Carmelo had last seen it. Red letters were missing from the large sign. The area that would normally serve as a mini-mart was empty: no cash register, no attendant, no chips, candy, or magazines, and no business. With so many people out of work and living in an environment so unstable, large corporations saw no reason to stick around. There was hardly a supermarket, fast food restaurant, or movie theatre in sight.

Jean Carmelo felt fortunate to have a sharp memory, but it was disheartening as well. In a strange way, Port-au-Prince reminded him of Washington D.C. Growing up, he assumed that a nation's capital would be one of its best kept cities. The glossy photos in his parochial school textbooks had made him want to either visit or live there someday. But in reality, the national monuments, D.C. was one of the most violent cities in the country. It was a mecca of urban poverty and drugs, especially during the 1990s. The National Palace in Haiti was a magnificent two-story building modeled after French Renaissance architecture in the 1700's. Its domed pavilion entrance and tall, regal columns were made of solid, white concrete. The lawns surrounding the building were on occasion as green and plush as the landscape in Washington. The scene outside the iron gates that kept the general public out was also an extreme opposite of the picture inside. Presidents and other political figures regularly practiced corruption.

Along their route, it was plain to see that unemployment and hardship had not been exaggerated. Centuries of slavery, unfair labor practices, American occupation, widespread government corruption, and lack of competent institutions had left Haiti one of the world's poorest countries. Yet, despite the overwhelming poverty, a small elite class existed, an insulated few who controlled a disproportionate share of the nation's wealth. This stark economic divide was not merely the result of misfortune but of deeply entrenched historical inequalities, political corruption, and limited opportunities for the majority. While the well-connected few lived in opulent homes behind high walls, the streets of Port-au-Prince teemed with people struggling to make ends meet.

Despite the ever-gloomy economic outlook, everybody seemed to have a destination. The high volume and pace of foot traffic were on par with midday in midtown Manhattan. Roadsides were flooded with scores of constantly moving people. Vendors with old wooden carts were posted in front of houses or closed businesses, selling goods ranging from generic toothpaste and beauty products to ice, water, and various foods. For them, survival depended on whatever commerce the day might bring.

A severely undernourished dog lay down on a flight of steps. Panting rapidly in the unforgiving heat, it wore an expression that seemed to question the necessity of enduring further torture, an unspoken reflection of the hardship that defined life for so many in the city.

The car was low on gas, so they stopped at one of the few gas stations that were actually open. The two pumps were occupied with a motorcycle and a jeep. While Jacques waited to use a pump, a group of boys knocked on the windshield. Seeking spare change, they offered to remove their dusty T-shirts to wipe the car. Instead, Jacques pulled up to the now-available pump, and an attendant filled the tank.

Jean Carmelo remembered the physical landmarks and the overall poverty of the people, but he had forgotten the constant carnival-parade atmosphere. In a month, the nearby city of Jacmel was preparing to throw the annual carnival. It was Haiti's largest celebration of the year. Haitians came from all over the world. The people here were already in rare form. The pulsating, booming bass, acoustic, and electric guitars of kompa music blasted from speakers, and the odor of rich, cooked food circulated in the air. But the urgency and despair in everyone's eyes quickly brought reality into sharper focus. If anyone was stationary, it wasn't because they were hanging out. They were watching what was going on around them, plotting their next move. Everyone's goal each and every day was survival.

When the Corolla got back on the road, Jean Carmelo kept absorbing as much of the scenery as he could. He had a flashback of when his uncle, Frantz, had taken him around town for frescos. Fresco carts had bells, similar to ice cream trucks back home, and a huge block of ice. All along the edges of the cart were colorful flavored syrups. The fresco man used a metal scraper to shave ice into small, medium, or large cups. Then the flavored syrup that the customer selected was poured on top of the shaved ice. On a hot day, there wasn't anything better. Jean Carmelo had a craving for one, but he didn't see any fresco vendors around.

As tight as it was with all five passengers bunched up inside the small sedan, Jean Carmelo's mind stayed charged and engaged. He saw so many attractive young women wearing next to nothing. His dad used to warn him about the high prevalence of prostitution, HIV, and other sexually transmitted diseases in Haiti. Jean Carmelo kept that front and center in his mind as he looked at the constant and seemingly accessible temptations walking the streets.

WELCOME BACK

A long white and blue banner hung from two telephone poles. It stretched from one side of the street to the other and read, "Bonne Fete, Carrefour!" *Happy Birthday, Carrefour!*

Residential buildings, open-air markets, bars, beauty salons, restaurants, produce stands, schools, and cargo transportation businesses lined the streets. Jean Carmelo and his family were entering the city of Carrefour, one of the more densely populated residential areas of Port-au-Prince. Boulevard Jean-Jacques Dessalines, was named after the leader who declared the country an independent nation after the Haitian Revolution. The road served as the capital's major artery and the only way for anyone looking to travel north or south. That was where Jean Carmelo's grandmother had lived her whole life. Hundreds of women and young girls walked along the roads with colorful baskets elegantly balanced on their heads. Filled with just about anything that could be bought or sold, those baskets served as effective transportation. As street vendors, they made enough money to feed their children. Young boys walked with blue five-gallon bottles of water on their shoulders. Old men sat around tables playing dominoes and checkers. Riders on worn bicycles and motorcyclists without helmets flowed up and down the busy streets.

Unless one was driving a sport utility vehicle or some sort of tank, auto maintenance would be a challenge. The roads were brutal. Sharp stones shot out from underneath tires in motion. The road that Jean Carmelo's grandmother had lived off of was cracked concrete pavement mixed with an assortment of rocks and sprinkled with numerous potholes. If a Haitian was fortunate enough to get his or her hands on a vehicle that moved, they rode it until something went wrong. Most of the vehicles were German or Japanese and built in the 80s or 90s. Thick black exhaust spewed out from vehicles all day long. The six foot-deep holes along the sides of the roads could cause problems during the day but could easily destroy any car or pedestrian once the sun went down. The Corolla pulled up in front of a house with a spiked, iron-gated entrance. Merchants were posted outside underneath a makeshift canopy, selling cooked, salty fish. When the gate opened, they were greeted by Jean Carmelo's uncle, Emmanuel; Anel, a close friend of the family;and Lauren, the housekeeper who had helped to care for Jean Carmelo's grandmother. All of them had played vital roles in keeping her going, and for that, he was grateful. They embraced with hugs and warm, open smiles.

"Ko man ou ye?" *How have you been?* Anel asked.

"Pa tro mal," *Not too bad,* Jean Carmelo replied.

"Sa fe lontan depi mwen pa wè w," *It's been such a long time since we've seen you,* Emmanuel said.

"Mwen kontan oue'w ou," *I'm happy to see you.* Jean Carmelo said.

Many people had said that Jean Carmelo and Emmanuel were obviously related. Emmanuel was in his late fifties and looked to be in good physical shape. He was shades lighter than Jean Carmelo and so laid back that he made Jean Carmelo appear high-strung. Anel was a bit younger than Emmanuel. He was active, always ready to fix a potential problem. When he spoke, he blinked rapidly and stammered every half dozen words or so. Emmanuel and Anel had barely aged after twelve years. Emmanuel grabbed some bags from the trunk and headed toward the house. Anel helped bring Jules down a concrete ramp that led to the short driveway in front of the garage and patio.

Jean Carmelo and Emmanuel took the rest of the bags inside. The house was just as he remembered it. It was a small, one-story cube built predominately from concrete. Years ago, his mom had talked about selling the house. Drawn in by its architectural simplicity, he had always wanted to go back to it, so he persuaded her to keep it.

He entered the small patio through the iron wire door. The design on the patio door allowed for plenty of air and sunlight to pass through. Insects and lizards were also free to roam in and out as they pleased. Many of the houses in that area had mosaic designs cut in the concrete instead of windows. Air conditioning was unheard of in that region. Dark brown tile led to the living room and dining room. A wooden door separated the patio from the interior. Once inside, Jean Carmelo noticed the beige suede sofas, covered in yellowed plastic that his parents had had when they lived in Brooklyn. The dusty streets made it impossible to keep anything looking new.

Jean Carmelo toured the hot—but cooler than outside—interior. He made his way to the back door to see the yard. Tall mango and palm trees shaded most of it. The yard wasn't wide, but it covered a good stretch of land. The ground was covered with white, grayish rocks and dirt. A handful of roosters and chickens roamed the yard, pecking at the ground for food.

In front of them, lying next to the sheet metal outhouse, were two dogs. They were some combination of mixed breed. He whistled to them, and they just looked at him as if he were crazy. Then out of the outhouse came a small black and beige puppy, no more than a few months old. He ran to Jean Carmelo with his ears up.

He knelt down to slap box with the puppy and rolled him around on the ground. The puppy was full of energy but had too many ribs showing for Jean Carmelo's liking. That would have to change while he was there.

When Anel showed up, he said that the other two dogs were the puppy's parents. The mother, who also had a black and beige short-haired coat, was the skinniest. She barely had the strength to stand without limping. When Jean Carmelo asked why the white-haired father was the only one with decent muscle tone, Anel told him how ruthless he was. On two separate occasions, he had eaten one of his offspring. As if he heard and understood them, the dog looked at Jean Carmelo and Anel. Jean Carmelo had a feeling that there was more to the story.

Out of all three of them, the puppy looked as though he wanted and needed the most attention. Jean Carmelo hadn't eaten the snack given to him on the airplane, so he tried to take his new buddy to the other side of the house where the other dogs wouldn't see them. When the other dogs noticed the pup's enthusiasm, they quickly came over.

The aroma of food being prepared came from the kitchen. They would eat soon, so Jean Carmelo decided to wait until later to feed the puppy. Dogs in that part of town weren't treasured as companions or playmates. Poverty and traditions passed down through generations reinforced the differences between humans and other animals. Dogs and cats co-existed with humans as long as they didn't interfere with the day-to-day activities. Jean Carmelo thought to himself. *Back in the states, pet owners set aside monthly and yearly budgets for their four-legged friends. There's the veterinarian check-ups, food, toys, clothes, appointments with dog sitters, dog walkers, photographers, obedience trainers, etc. The closest thing dogs around here have to toys is hard rocks and rotting tree branches. Most are lucky if they are able to drink water from leaky, garden hoses.* If there was a limited amount of food in a household, the unwanted scraps went to the pets. Having a dog meant protection or security. They provided surveillance and were restricted from entering the home. If a dog couldn't or wouldn't bite a potential threat, then it at least had to bark and warn its owner when a stranger was on the property. If it did not fulfill those duties consistently, it was considered useless. Useless dogs were found aimlessly roaming the streets until they succumbed to starvation, disease, or the elements.

TAP TAP

The streets of Carrefour were loud with chatter, motors, and the loud music from house speakers and tap taps. Tap taps, privately owned vehicles, were the only form of public transportation. Tap tap meant "quick quick" in creole. Drivers would charge a few cents to anyone looking to ride in their pick-up trucks or buses. Some observed regular routes, but for the most part, passengers got in wherever they fit.

Once they got on, they told the driver, "Ale!" – *Go!* When passengers reached their destinations, they would yell, "Rete!" – *Stay!*

The tap taps were painted with the brightest colors and extravagant designs, meant to draw in business. Some drivers would pay big money to have their vehicles painted numerous times per year. Although Jean Carmelo had only ridden one a half-dozen times, they had formed an impression on him. Popular rappers, singers, religious and political figures, or whoever the driver thought was relevant would get hand-painted on the sides. One of his favorite tap taps had a mural of Tupac with the words "Only God Can Judge Me" written above it. There were cliché Kreyol phrases or well-known pictures and slogans from American pop culture written in large letters. The paintings allowed customers to tell them apart and take a better gamble on the mechanical maintenance of each vehicle. The main ingredient that brought in the most customers was the music. The tap taps that consistently had standing room only were the ones with the cleanest sound systems and best selection of kompa. People that didn't know each other would sing and laugh together on route cross-town. Dozens of tap taps filled the crowded streets, blaring music that served as the city's audio backdrop.

The scent of charcoal smoke signaled that Lauren had finished preparing lunch. The dogs ate cornmeal, rice, and bones out back. Everyone took turns washing their hands. There was no running water, so a large plastic container on the top of the house captured rain water. The sun-warmed water was put in buckets and brought into the house, and cups in the bathroom were used to make managing the water easier.

The family sat around the table next to a refrigerator. The table was dressed with cutlery, plates, cups, wine bottles filled with Culligan water, and bowls of hot food. Sitting at the table brought back memories of Jean Carmelo's first communion, high school graduation, birthday parties, and the dinners he'd shared with his mom and dad as a kid. He took in the pleasant scent of the meal and became aware of how hungry he was. Someone must have spread the word beforehand, because Lauren had prepared diri ak sòs pwa—*rice with bean sauce*. It was his favorite dish, especially when completed with pwason or poul—*fish* or *chicken*—and legume—*vegetables*.

No matter how many times he'd had that dish before, it tasted much different in Port-au-Prince. The most obvious difference was the meat. The chicken was tender and caught his taste buds off guard. Only his mom and dad understood English, so when Rose noticed his grin, she asked him what was funny. He found it amusing that everyone's undivided attention was focused on their plates. It wasn't a rude gesture on anyone's part; they went a long time between meals.

After the meal, Jean Carmelo went out toward the front gate. The noise from the cars and trucks blasting their horns did not cease. It was loud, but a welcome change from his regular pace of life. Across the street was a two-story building with a small business on the bottom floor. The owner opened the doors to a waiting line of people looking to buy water, beauty supplies, toothpaste, alcohol, phone cards, and a dozen other goods. On the second floor was another business of some sort. A tall, pretty girl, her hair in a ponytail, worked on the balcony. She looked at Jean Carmelo and smiled before turning toward a voice that was calling her inside.

Emmanuel and Anel came over to catch up. Even though they had only met each other a handful of times, they all enjoyed learning about each other's cultures. They told Jean Carmelo about what life had been like after the hurricanes and tropical storms hit their country. Aside from the more visible damage, the land had suffered.

Emmanuel said, scratching his head, "La vi ya vi n pi mal. Se premyé fwa moun yo wè bagay sa yo." *The living and working conditions here have only gotten worse.*

The grim reality was that most of the inhabitants would not accomplish half of what they were capable of. With so few job opportunities available, owning a home appeared nearly impossible to many who lived there. Jean Carmelo's Kreyol hadn't improved much. He communicated with a mixture of Kreyol, French, English, and makeshift sign language. That was more than enough for him to get his points across and for them to understand each other fairly easily.

Jean Carmelo asked them, "Eské nou pansé nou ka ale viv aux Eta Zini?" *Do you two ever think about coming to live in the United States?*

"Non, nou pap jan'm kité Ayiti paské nou pli alèz la," *No, this is where we are from and we feel more comfortable here.* Anel said.

Haitians were attached by more than just gravitational pull. Their unique blend of history, culture, and unmistakable features kept millions from leaving. They were direct descendants of freedom fighters. Their ancestors fought and died to complete the world's largest and most successful slave rebellion in 1804. They were the first free black republic in the world. But this hard-won freedom came at a devastating price. France, the former colonial power, demanded reparations from Haiti for the "property" lost by former slaveholders, the enslaved people themselves. Under threat of reinvasion and international isolation, Haiti agreed to pay an indemnity that would cripple the young nation for generations. Over 122 years, until 1947, Haiti transferred what would amount to more than $21 billion in today's currency to France. During some periods, up to 80% of Haiti's national income went toward servicing this unjust debt, resources that should have built schools, hospitals, and infrastructure instead flowed to the very nation that had enslaved them. Despite this extraordinary economic burden, pride ran deep in their blood. Emmanuel and Anel weren't interested in the States, and who could judge them?

Rose's mother had always stressed education to her children, so Emmanuel had learned construction. His skills lost their value over the years in the shifting economic and political climate. Every now and then, he worked on small projects with a group of friends he'd gone to school with. Anel, fidgeting with an orange cell phone, had never known his family. He enjoyed transforming malfunctioning electronic gadgets into works of art. Like more than half of the people in Haiti, he had not attended school, spoke Kreyol, and was functionally illiterate. Yet Emmanuel and Anel still had hope that one day things could change. In Jean Carmelo's mind, that ideology was a bit of a stretch.

The pup hopped in Jean Carmelo's direction and jumped up to nibble at his ankles. He still had the snacks from the flight in his pocket, and the other dogs weren't around. He pulled out the box of wheat saltines, a small round white cheese, raisins, and dark chocolate. He knelt down, broke the saltines into smaller pieces, and invited the puppy to eat from his hand. The pup leaned in closer and sniffed but wouldn't eat. When Jean Carmelo dropped the food onto the ground, the pup quickly ate it up. He wondered why the pup would behave like that. He looked at Anel and saw his puzzled expression.

Jean Carmelo asked, "Pouki sa mwen pa jan'm oue'w ap joue avèk chyen yo?" *Why don't I ever see you playing with the dogs?*

"Lè yo piti, yo bezwen mou'n man yen yo jwé avèk yo, bay manje. Lè yo vin gwo, yo pa bezoin moun ankò." *They like people when they are puppies and they need you, but they don't show the same level of joy when they grow into adult dogs.*

Jean Carmelo said, "Se pa vre! Dépi wou okipé yo byen, yap toujou rinmen w min m lè yo vi n gran." *That's not true! If you treat them right when they're puppies, just the opposite will be true when they mature.*

Anel didn't seem to buy his argument. Jean Carmelo also noticed that whenever he opened the patio door and stepped into the house, no matter how excited the pup was, he wouldn't follow. The puppy acted as if an invisible force-field were stopping him. His grandma had liked dogs, but like most Haitians, she hadn't tolerated them in the house. The pup must have instinctively known what his boundaries were.

Lights Out

It was beginning to get dark. Jean Carmelo unpacked his bags in the living room area where he would be sleeping. As tired as he was, the energy from the street drew him in. Men and women were socializing at the bars, dancing and living in the moment. Festive melodies and rhythms blasted throughout the town, communicating a sense of joy and well-being that Jean Carmelo had not witnessed anywhere else.

On his way to the front gate, Jean Carmelo saw Jules in a metal chair looking out at the street. Jean Carmelo turned around, went inside, and came back with a matching metal chair. He placed it next to Jules. He was having more and more trouble coming to terms with no longer being able to connect with his dad.

"What are you thinking about?" Jean Carmelo asked while squealing brakes and engines provided background filler.

"What did you say?" Jules asked.

"You look like you're thinking deeply about something," Jean Carmelo said, raising his voice to carry over the noise.

"I don't know why they have to play the music so loud!" Jules said, referring to the tap taps.

"That's the only way they can survive and keep their business going."

"Sitting too close to speakers will break your ears." Jules shook his head in disagreement.

Jules had a valid point, and that was a statement he would've made years ago. Traces of his vintage personality were intact. Jean Carmelo was happy to see Jules responding to the change in environment. Since Jules's interactions were more fluid in Kreyol, Jean Carmelo wanted to believe his father's brain would engage more actively in a familiar setting. They watched the street action for a while before a collective sigh flared from the crowds.

The power abruptly went out. It became completely dark, except for the headlights from the vehicles. Jean Carmelo stood and held his cell phone high, using the bright light to walk inside and see where everyone else was.

Anel came out of his room with a flashlight. "I know where the Delco is."

A few minutes later, Anel walked into the living room with a gasoline-powered portable machine. Emmanuel brought some gas in in a plastic milk container and filled up the machine's tank. After pulling on a cord similar to one used to start a lawn mower, Anel got the motor running. The lights in the living room and patio slowly flickered back on.

Most sections of Port-au-Prince received only a couple of hours of electricity every other day or every two to three days. There hadn't been a set schedule for decades, and most of the electric circuits in the house had been broken for years. That was why the refrigerator in the dining room had empty shelves and a wide-open door. Most generators ran on gasoline, which didn't come cheap and didn't last long. Even with cash to burn, most foods, especially perishables, had to be bought from street vendors on a daily basis. Most Haitians couldn't remember a time when they'd experienced several consecutive days of power. Some believed that the electricity was shut off to encourage people to stay indoors and off the streets.

The crowds on the street paused momentarily to acknowledge the loss of power, but they were used to the routine. The music from the vehicles kept on, and more than a few homeowners had generators to keep their power going.

Jean Carmelo had officially hit the wall and was ready to crash for the night. He walked inside and asked Rose what bed he would be sleeping on.

She pointed at a folded-up bed a few feet over. "You can use that bed. That's grandma's bed."

He was caught by surprise and didn't know what to say. She must have noticed his hesitation.

"Those sheets have been washed and pressed, or you can use these. I don't think they fit that bed though," she said calmly.

One look at the other sheets was enough to determine that they wouldn't fit the twin sized bed.

"Okay, good night, Mom. I'll see you in the morning," he said.

Jean Carmelo had never been overly superstitious, but sleeping in his grandmother's bed was strange... in a good way. No one had used it since she left. He was honored.

The legs had small wheels on them, so he pushed the bed over by the front door. He climbed in and sat cross-legged to meditate, calmly soaking up everything living around him. It had been a long, packed day. He was looking forward to seeing more of the country the next day.

The temperature cooled down considerably overnight. He slept well and woke to the cadence and lusty tenor of roosters crowing their morning gospels. Ten minutes after five a.m., he got out of bed to brush his teeth and wash his face. He had been waking up at that hour for years.

He performed his morning ritual of push-ups and drank a glass of water out on the patio. Waking up before sunrise gave him an unmatched sense of freedom and humbleness that he had always cherished.

Years ago, his brother Augustin would come home to visit for a few weeks between overseas stints in the Army. He was enthusiastic about physical fitness and would wake Jean Carmelo up to join him on the local track. Jean Carmelo had thought that his brother was missing a few screws. Jean Carmelo was more into afternoon romps of bicycle motocross. He dreaded going out into the chilly morning frost when dew still clung to the tips of the grass. The dreariness in his eyes, the numbness in his brain, and the whistling wheeze of asthma in his lungs felt awful. He still couldn't figure out why, but for some reason, he had continued the practice of waking early for years. Jean Carmelo was officially an early bird.

It was so peaceful at that time of the morning. He had looked forward to an escape from the technology that many times became a distraction. He'd brought his iPod but hadn't used it since touching down in Florida. With no access to a television or computer, he couldn't monitor the clock, waiting to receive or send an email. Only an emergency would make him accept the roaming fees on his cell phone. There was a small portable radio by the front door, but he had no desire to turn it on. The background noise of the wildlife was a welcome change.

Anel woke up not long after and did a double take when he saw Jean Carmelo. He told Jean Carmelo that he had long held the title for getting up the earliest. He had thought Jean Carmelo was a tourist who would easily sleep for nine or more hours.

"Se lè sa-a mwen leve chak matin," *This is the time that I wake up every morning.* Jean Carmelo said.

"Wou grangou?" *Are you hungry?* Anel asked.

He planned to go buy food once the rest of the family got up. Everyone had already made up their minds the night before on what they wanted for breakfast. Anel focused his attention on the street. His short-sleeved polo shirt and grey khakis were worn but not dirty. People there, no matter how poor, wore their best clothes when they left the house to go anywhere. Many people passing by knew Anel and greeted him and Jean Carmelo.

"Da-m ki van n zé, zonyon et pén ap vini ta lè la." *The woman who sells bread, eggs, and onions will come around here shortly.*

Certain vendors would come by each day at the same time. Anel knew where and when to find them all. As each hour passed, an additional layer of audio would add on. By 8 a.m., the scene outside was as hectic as it had been the night before. There were no alternate routes for people heading toward the beaches or for the various trucks transporting commerce. Anel and Jean Carmelo decided to hit the road and track down what they needed.

Jean Carmelo had no idea what the proper price was to pay for anything, so he tagged along and observed. Vendors shouted out what they were selling and what they were selling them for. Some had carts lined with combs, mirrors, hair gels, and other beauty aids. Anel saw a woman balancing a basket of bread on her head. She passed the woman sitting off to the side of the road selling chickens and eggs. When they stopped her, they carried out two missions almost simultaneously. Carrying their inventory from one side of town to the other was an incredible amount of work for the vendors, so one could hardly blame them for sticking to their prices amid customers trying to bargain them down. After a bit of legwork, Jean Carmelo and Anel got everything they'd set out for and headed back.

They'd worked up a decent appetite by the time they returned. When they opened the front gate, the puppy was lying on his mother's side. He saw who was entering the property and trotted over to greet Jean Carmelo and Anel. He did some kind of circling dance of joy and sniffed Jean Carmelo's shoelaces. Jean Carmelo passed the bread and eggs to Anel as he went inside, and Jean Carmelo stayed outside to play with the furry ball of energy.

Jean Carmelo had already noticed the contrast between the strong family culture in Haiti and the loose style he practiced at home. His grandmother had instilled in all her children the importance of discipline and communication. She made it a strict rule that meals were shared together at the table. In less than twenty-four hours, his immediate family was sitting down to eat together for a second time. That simply didn't happen in the States.

When Lauren was done preparing breakfast, she invited everyone to gather around. Jean Carmelo ordinarily ate egg whites only. He remembered all the times he'd ordered egg white sandwiches at a deli, and without a second thought, the yokes were thrown away. Throwing away anything edible just didn't make sense in Port-au-Prince.

Small ceramic bowls of boiled plantains, along with hard dough bread, were passed around the table. The bread was his favorite. It had a tough but soft spongy feel, and he could have easily eaten every loaf they brought that morning. They talked about everything from Haiti's current political condition to its chances of ever putting together a football team that would surpass their 1974 World Cup squad.

The dogs barked out front, indicating that someone was trying to enter the yard. It was George, Rose's sister Claudette, and her friend Felecia. They'd come by to take Rose to another sister's house a dozen blocks over. George was an upbeat and energetic young man. He made himself at home, walking around, greeting everyone, shaking the hands of the men, and giving the women pecks on the cheek.

Rose didn't want anyone feeling uncomfortable, so she asked them, "Eské wou vle manjé avèk nou?" *Do you want to eat with us?*

"Non, nou manjé avan nou vi n la...g in inè d tan de sa," *No, we ate an hour before we got here.* The two women replied.

"Mwen pa ka di non paské manjé ya santi tè l man bon. Wi, map manjé yon ti kal," *I can't pass on food that smells this good. Yes, I would like to eat a little bit.* George replied, smiling and rubbing his belly.

Rose invited him to sit and eat. He sat in the available chair next to Jules, and Lauren brought him a placemat and some silverware.

"Méda'm pi ga ou pran pòz étrangé. Meté kò' nou alèz," *Ladies, don't act like strangers. Make yourselves at home.* Rose said, pointing toward the living room.

"Merci," they replied.

Claudette and Felecia sat on the sofa chairs across from the dining room table. In between mouthfuls, George recalled earlier times when he'd come to visit. He seemed to enjoy the meal.

When everyone was done, Rose asked Jean Carmelo if he wanted to tag along for the ride. He figured that if there was room for him, he would go. He was getting a little bored, and he didn't want to stay inside more than he had to. Jules would have Lauren and Anel to keep an eye on him. Jean Carmelo stepped outside to join the others at the front where their ride was waiting. Blinking in the bright sunshine, he remembered to run back inside to get his cell phone, digital camera, and gulp down one last glass of water.

When they were all ready to go, the six of them crammed into a rust-colored, 1990 Isuzu Rodeo. For some strange reason, Rose said she had to sit in the front passenger seat.

Jean Carmelo asked puzzled and slightly annoyed. "Mom, are you serious? They live here."

"Yes, but George doesn't know the address. I have to give directions!" she insisted.

He didn't understand, but reluctantly squeezed in the back with Emmanuel, Claudette, and Felecia. He couldn't decide if it was tougher to fit into that car or the one from the airport. Jean Carmelo and his friends in the States frequently made fun of cars filled beyond capacity. He never thought he'd be in that position himself.

The streets of Port-au-Prince were buzzing with the normal midday traffic. As they drove off, he was amazed at how desensitized the pedestrians were to the cars and heavy trucks moving so close to them. They looked as though they were aware of the vehicles proximity to them, but they had a higher tolerance for near misses.

Jean Carmelo held on to the front passenger seat and concentrated on preventing his head from smashing against the window. He accomplished that by keeping a keen eye on the road to see where the next ditch or large rock was. Unfortunately, there were plenty. The hills and tight turns would have made it an uncomfortable ride in the best of circumstances, but that ride was just plain painful for everyone in the back. He noticed George and the other drivers sounding their horns yards before they approached intersections.

"Viré a goch nan lòt riyel la," *Make a left turn at the next corner.* Rose told George.

There were no stop signs or traffic lights, and the narrow streets did not allow for much visibility. Tall, concrete walls surrounding the edges of many of the corner properties didn't make things any easier. Thrill seekers were still willing to take chances, California-rolling through intersections. So many vehicles were not maintained properly. Drivers would run cars with faulty brakes, well past-worn tires, or other compromised vital parts. Jean Carmelo was truly amazed at how those people continued to persevere.

SOUKE

As they turned onto the correct block, they all focused on finding the yellow house with the blue gate. That block was much quieter. A small group of adolescent kids kicked a deflated soccer ball, moving out of the road when they noticed the approaching vehicle.

The jeep arrived at a property with two two-story buildings surrounded by a concrete wall with a blue iron gate. Spaced an inch apart on top of the concrete wall were primary-colored iron spikes. George got out first and assisted the passengers on the driver's side by folding down the driver's seat. He then came around to help Rose out the jeep. When he folded down the front passenger seat to let everyone else through, Jean Carmelo practically fell out. His legs were numb and stiff as wooden pegs. He couldn't take much more of the sardine-style transportation. He helped Claudette and Felecia out after him.

Dominique, Rachelle, Renee, and their children greeted the group at the front gate. Rose reintroduced Jean Carmelo to her sisters Rachelle and Renee, and they introduced him to their children. Their faces seemed familiar. Carol, Jacob, Rachelle, and Gabrielle were all in his mom's family photo albums.

"Mes-z-amis! Sil vous plait, entré an n dan. Il fait chaud," *My goodness! Please come inside. It's terribly hot outside,* Dominique said, shaking his head.

They all stepped inside. A sofa lined the wall farthest from the front door. It was similar to the one at Jean Carmelo's grandmother's house, complete with the thick plastic cover. A small glass table stood in between the sofa and the two white plastic chairs Rose and Jean Carmelo sat in.

The women began conversing in French. Jean Carmelo tried to think of something he could do to pass the time, but where could he go? Even though he had taken numerous French classes, Jean Carmelo felt much more comfortable listening to Kreyol.

Dominique came in and noticed Jean Carmelo's boredom. He called him outside and offered to show him around the place. Dominique adjusted his eye glasses and grabbed a set of keys from a hook on the wall. They proceeded up the concrete stairs outside, and he directed Jean Carmelo to where the classrooms were. Jean Carmelo hadn't noticed the sign out front that said the building was a school.

Dominique asked, "Eské ou palé Kréyol?" *Do you speak Kreyol?*

"Kreyol mwen pa trò bon," *My Kreyol is not too good,* Jean Carmelo replied.

"I'm the director and principal of this grade school," Dominique said. "What did you study in school?"

"I majored in English," Jean Carmelo answered. "I'm a writer working in the banking industry right now. I'm doing what I have to do in this recession."

"Keep following where your passion leads you, and I assure you that you will get another chance to do what your talents have put you here to do," Dominique said.

His encouragement seemed sincere, and Jean Carmelo appreciated it. Dominique opened a door and showed him where the kids had their classes. It was after three p.m., so all the classrooms were empty. Each grade from kindergarten to sixth had its own room, and each classroom was kept immaculate. There were neat rows of wood-and-metal tables and chairs. The double-sided chalkboards on wheels were wiped. The chalk was placed in its box on the accessory tray. The floors were so clean they looked as though they had been freshly painted. Jean Carmelo couldn't help but laugh when they looked into the kindergarteners' room. He tried to remember when his legs could fit comfortably under desks that small.

Next, they walked over to the secretary's office. The secretary handled the attendance and tuition duties. Jean Carmelo asked Dominique if there was a nurse's office. That had been his home away from home as a grade-schooler. Dominique told him that if a child needed medical attention, they had a first aid kit and easy access to a vehicle to transport them to the hospital.

They advanced through a maze of other rooms, and before long, they were back in the living room. Jean Carmelo had great respect for the fortitude, commitment, and hard work it took to run a successful school. Dominique offered to bring everyone some pineapple soda. Before he sat back down, Jean Carmelo spotted two Casio digital keyboards standing up in the far corner of the room. He asked who played the keys.

"Jakòb la pran kèk leson pyano. Li jwe pou l'égliz avec lékol li," *Jacob's taking some piano lessons. He also plays for the church and his school,* Jacob's mother, Rachelle, said.

"Mwen bezoin oue'w kap jwé," *I want to watch you play,* Jacob said with a smile.

"Mwen pa jwe telman byen. Mwen apran-n son plot avèk zòrèy mwen," *I don't play that well. I play sounds by ear,* Jean Carmelo replied.

He tried to explain to Jacob that he made instrumental beats by auditioning sounds and putting them together. Jacob asked him to demonstrate—either because he didn't understand or he didn't want to believe him.

Carol came back with a tray full of glasses with ice cubes and pineapple champagne soda. Besides his annual bottle of Dr. Pepper, pineapple soda was the only soda Jean Carmelo liked. He took a glass and a napkin and placed them on the low wooden table. He grabbed a keyboard and placed it on his lap. It had more keys than his Juno, so he got a little excited. Jacob got the AC adaptor to plug it into the wall, and Jean Carmelo pressed the power button. They actually had electricity!

He turned a few knobs and played preset sounds on the keys. Then he ran through some basic random patterns using the pads and string sections, which didn't sound too bad. He passed the keyboard over to Jacob so he could drink his soda. The heat from outside clashed with the ice cubes fighting to keep his drink cold. Jean Carmelo listened to Jacob play. *This kid is all right!*

Rose, who was sitting beside him, told the room about when she'd signed Jean Carmelo up for piano lessons. He'd taken classes at a small school down the block from where they lived on E. 92nd Street in East Flatbush.

"Le'l te gin sept ans, mwen te min nin kay yon vwazin aba yo profese ki lap monte'l joue piano." *When he was seven, I took him down the street to a piano teacher for a couple of years.* She said that was short-lived though, because the Marcelin family who'd lived upstairs didn't appreciate that kind of noise.

A menacing rumble with more force than dozens of high-speed locomotives came straight at them...from every possible direction. In that first fraction of a second, Jean Carmelo felt an alien sensation - electricity both surrounding and moving through his body, a primal force emanating from the earth itself. The building oscillated rapidly and violently, throwing them onto the floor as if they were life-sized dolls.

From deep below came a sound he had never heard before and would never forget - a deep, bass-like grinding of rocks shifting beneath their feet, as if the planet's bones were being crushed. The sound grew louder, more intense, combining with ear-splitting, cataclysmal mayhem that came in what felt like multiple three-second intervals.

His body responded before his mind could process what was happening. Pure instinct drove him into a deep squat position, his muscles fighting against the chaotic waves surging up through his legs with continuous, uniform pressure. His eyes darted everywhere but fixed mainly straight ahead, desperately searching for balance as the ground beneath them rippled and bucked.

Time seemed to both compress and expand. The cups and glasses on the table shattered against the walls and floor. Green and red Haitian dollar bills sprayed from Rose's purse like confetti. The electric charge from the earth made it impossible to move freely - every action had to be intuitive, automatic, driven by survival instincts he didn't know he possessed.

Jean Carmelo looked up and noticed wooden shelves and chips of paint and concrete being spit from the ceiling. The deepest corridors of his mind were like Rubik's Cubes, twisting between vivid flashbacks and the present. Subconscious visions of September 11, 2001, in New York fueled his confusion. Who would attack this country now? What more can they want from the poor?

Through the chaos, he heard distressed voices crying their last wishes, dying in the distance. Waves of electric energy kept the room violently shaking at distinct speeds. These were unique combinations of erratic movements he had never felt before. He smelled wide pools of concentrated fear, which would soon mix with an acrid, metallic odor - the terrible smell of death from neighboring buildings seeping through the air.

The women and children around him were shielding their faces and heads, kneeling and screaming.

"Jezi! Jezi!" Jesus! Jesus! They shouted.

Immersed in an abyss of terror, he heard blood-curdling screams. People yelled, "Anmwe! Anmwe!" Help! Help!

Then came a moment of absolute silence. Jean Carmelo froze in place, his body rigid with tension. In those few eternal seconds, his thoughts raced to his family members who weren't with them. The silence was broken by new sounds of destruction - buildings collapsing, people screaming, chaos erupting in every direction.

Thin grey dust began filling the air, its texture visible in the shafts of light still penetrating the room. It coated his skin and gradually worked its way into his mouth and nose, making each breath more challenging than the last. The dust moved through the air like a passing cloud of despair, shifting from dark to light grey as it caught what remained of the day's illumination.

Everything felt damaged, covered in a layer of pulverized concrete. The building that had provided them with shelter just moments ago now threatened to become their tomb. This was more than an earthquake - it was a complete assault on every human sense, a moment when the solid ground beneath their feet betrayed them and the world itself seemed to be tearing apart.

Blocks away, Jules sat motionless on the bed in the bedroom while the world around him shook. Facing the window, he stared outside with barely an expression. He had reached yet another of life's forks in the road.

In his mind, that was the best of both worlds. He chose his fate without effort. The crashing noise was a nasty storm that he would blend in with. There was calmness in his demeanor. He seemed content with whatever this amazing muscle had in store. It was as if he had been waiting for this moment to arrive. He thought to himself, *Jehovah is here. He must be very angry. No more pain...no more suffering. Now, we can all go in peace.*

Tall, concrete walls began to tumble around him. The dogs howled and yawned while hunching their bodies. They trembled with tails tucked between their rear legs in trepidation. Jules held on tight to the headboard. He said nothing. He heard random screams and pleas for forgiveness from people in the streets. Someone called his name. The roof above him made a cracking sound. He saw a light. He saw the end.

Back on the other side of town, a beam of light coming from the open door begged Jean Carmelo to come closer. His affinity for sunlight allowed him to relax. He dashed toward it, looked outside, and saw a dark, grey haze. He looked back into the living room. Rose was the closest person to him. She was on her knees, crying in prayer, when he grabbed her under her arms.

"We've gotta get outside the building now!" he shouted, narrowing his eyes.

"Jezi! Jezi!" she yelled, her head tilted back as she tried to anchor herself to the floor.

He allowed instinct to guide him. He lifted her off her knees and dragged her to the door. The thundering crunch of concrete, steel, and snapping trees stirred another burst of screams. Something humongous had just fallen next door. That, combined with a sudden slow dimming of light, told him the building could collapse and trap them. The ground finally stood still. Jean Carmelo saw that as their chance! He and Rose were underneath the door pane, which was the strongest part of the building.

Rose yelled at Jean Carmelo, "Don't go outside!" She pointed at a telephone pole that was leaning in their direction.

Although her concern was valid, he had already made up his mind that he would not allow anything to land on them. "I see it. It won't come down on us."

He looked into his mom's eyes, trying to reassure her that they would be okay.

"Leve ate ya!" *Get up off the floor!*, He commanded.

"We've gotta get moving."

"Fo nou kite kounie ya," *We must leave now!* Rose added.

Two of her daughters helped Renee off the floor and to her walker. Jean Carmelo felt something glued to his fingers. He stared in disbelief at the empty drinking glass still in his left hand. He took a quick head count and heard voices coming from the second floor.

"Are you all right?" Jean Carmelo called.

"Yes, I'm okay!" Dominique replied. He came down the stairs looking startled, but he didn't have any visible physical damage.

No one knew what had just hit them. They all walked outside, embracing and consoling each other and looking around. Dominique and Jean Carmelo ventured to the front gate.

People from a few houses down walked out into the street, hands clasped over their heads, screaming, "Difé! Difé!" *Fire! Fire!*

Their houses were on fire, and no water was available to put out the flames. Thick black circles of smoke shot out from behind the gray, dusty backdrop. People were walking in the streets, searching for what had happened. The loud crashing sound they had heard from the building next door was a large portion of the second floor that had dropped to the ground, crushing a motor scooter and its rider.

Jean Carmelo remembered that he had his camera. He pulled it out and snapped a few shots. Feeling restricted by the small digital screen, he put it away and took in his natural panoramic view. A large four-story building directly across the street, still under construction, had lost huge chunks of concrete and cinder blocks.

Jean Carmelo stood tall and confident, looking in every direction for an answer. He knew that mental attitude was the key. Allowing everyone around him to feed off of his positive energy would be crucial to their survival. He couldn't see any planes or craters. An atomic bomb would've probably killed all of them.

Dominique and Jean Carmelo warned the women and kids not to go back inside and to stay away from power lines, trees, and buildings. Screams, loud cries, and car alarms sounded all around them. The magnitude of the situation was becoming more and more clear. Jean Carmelo remembered that his mom had her cell phone. Jules, Anel and Lauren were still on the other side of town, and their whereabouts and well-being darted around Jean Carmelo's mind.

He asked Rose, "Ma, where's your phone?"

She searched her pockets. "It must have fallen somewhere inside."

Carol had her phone. She used Digicel as her provider, and she tried to make a call. But she couldn't get a dial tone. The phone service was out of commission. Jean Carmelo had a feeling that that was only the beginning of the endless concerns he would have throughout their ordeal.

Wide-eyed people sped past on mopeds. Others walked up and down the street, delivering doomsday gospels. "Sa se la fin du mond!" *The end of the world is here!* A woman, no older than forty, walked up holding her young daughter's hand and a small, unframed picture of her son. She asked everyone but no one had seen him.

Jean Carmelo heard plastic scraping on the ground behind him, and he walked over to see what it was. Dominique had gone back inside the house to get white plastic chairs, a flashlight, and a small radio.

"I didn't even see you leave!" Jean Carmelo said.

"I figured that because I know where everything is in this house, I should get some things for us," he replied.

Jean Carmelo helped him bring several chairs over to the group. They placed them in two neat rows along the edge of the street and sat.

Before they could collectively exhale, a grumbling eruption approached them again. They shared a communal gasp, preparing their bodies for impact as the earth shook up and down, side to side. Rose grabbed Jean Carmelo's hand and squeezed it as hard as she could.

"All right! All right! We're okay." He said to no one in particular while looking around for any objects that could harm them. He noticed some odd cloud formations.

Six excruciatingly long seconds later, the trembling stopped. *How long would this continue?* Headlights shined on them as cars drove past. With a feather-light touch, Dominique rolled the radio dial back and forth, patiently searching for reception. After exhausting all the options on the AM stations, he switched to FM. Finally, he came across a louder signal. It faded in and out, but it sounded like music. When the sound became audible, Jean Carmelo recognized the song. It was "Hotel California" by the Eagles. One of the lyrics in the song said, "you can check out anytime you like, but you can never leave". It was a song about how a beautiful place can quickly become a nightmare. He didn't follow any religion but Jean Carmelo wondered. *Was this some special message being sent to them?* With no other choices to turn the dial to, they left the radio on. For some reason, the same song played over and over.

Everything and everyone around them had changed. They were suddenly living in a different world. The mystery of what would happen next was unbearable. Cries and yells blended together. Every few minutes, a distressed individual on the verge of total emotional breakdown would walk or run by. Dogs and cats cowered close to the ground. Chickens, roosters and ponies roamed the streets as if they would not rest until they located a safe haven. The loud squeak from a dog in a two-story building next to them was difficult to ignore. Its pleas could be heard for some distance.

As the sun made its final curtain call, slowly disappearing, Jean Carmelo felt as though he were losing one of his closest friends. Something told him its warm rays weren't gone forever, but under what circumstances would they meet again? The temperature slid down at an accelerated rate. Jean Carmelo started to think about going back into the house to get supplies for the night.

"How are you feeling?" he asked Rose.

"A little light-headed," she replied.

"What did you bring with you?"

"I had a black bag with my insulin in it."

He had to go back inside to get it. He thought that he had the speed to get in and out before the building collapsed. He stood to go back in.

"Jean Carmelo, take this with you." Dominique handed him a flashlight.

"What else do we need?" Jean Carmelo asked.

"You won't know where things are. I'll go if we need anything else. Please be careful." Dominique answered.

Jean Carmelo used the flashlight to find his way to the front gate entrance, which was about forty yards away. He fiddled with the gate lock and tried to find a handle or some sort of latch. After a few minutes, he finally got the latch to click open by reaching through the gate. All of his senses were on high sensitivity.

He walked through the front door and spotted the bag right away. Jean Carmelo snatched it up and looked around the living room to assess the damage. Chairs and tables were broken, glass was shattered everywhere, papers and pens were peppered throughout, and chips of concrete had been sprinkled lightly over the sofa.

It was time to leave. He had gotten what he had come for, so he made his way through the front door and rejoined the group. He was amazed by how just hours ago, those same walls had provided them with comfort and security. Now they were weapons shooting debris and crushing people underneath tons of earth and concrete.

Hours later.

They stayed silent as their attention focused on a voice coming from the radio.

"Nou fe yon esperyans nan trambléman de terre." *We have just experienced a major earthquake.* The speaker identified the station as

Signal FM 90.5. He said that reports were claiming that the impressive show of fury was either a 7.0 or 7.3. "Yo panes kon byen mile moun mouri." *Hundreds of thousands of people have been presumed dead.* "Gin yon paket kiloamba de kombe." *Many others are trapped underneath buildings.*

Looking at each other in disbelief, they realized how fortunate they were to be alive. The speaker went on about the strength and potential damage of earthquakes. He said that a 7.3 and 7.0 sounded like they were similar, but a 7.3 was far more dominant. Only a handful of earthquakes on record had ever caused that much destruction. The speaker described the shaking that occurred after the first earthquake as an aftershock.

"Se possib nou tonjou ap pran sekous trambleman de terre..." *It may be possible for these aftershocks to continue for days, weeks or even...*

Right on cue, the earth trembled again for several seconds. The aftershock had less muscle than the previous two shakes, but the threat of disaster was no less. The unpredictability of the sudden jolts made everyone uncomfortable. The most humbling feeling was accepting that they were vulnerable to a force much greater than them.

The radio offered a quick education about aftershocks. It was possible that a mightier, more destructive quake could follow the initial tremor. After they heard that, they couldn't help but jump every time they felt another quake. The speaker described the last earthquake to hit Port-au-Prince. A 7.5 had hit in 1770, killing a couple hundred people. An earthquake that shook the Dominican Republic in 1946 had affected parts of Haiti with a tsunami that killed over a thousand people.

Tsunami sounded the same in English as it did in Kreyol. When Jean Carmelo heard that word, he asked for a clear-cut translation and listened with heightened attention. The speaker said that some national warning center had issued a tsunami warning for all of Port-au-Prince. As much as he didn't want to believe what he had heard, he knew he'd understood correctly. He had remembered the tsunami in Indonesia years earlier. One picture in particular showed dozens of people looking up at one a one-hundred-foot-high wave. He used to think those waves were only seen in "end of the world" movies.

Jean Carmelo knew that they were in for a long night. The good news was that they were given another chance to breathe and find ways to keep living. The women huddled together, consoling one another and keeping the kids from breaking down. Periodically, they would take the flashlight and go away from the rest of the group to crouch down and pee. The frequency of their trips indicated their high levels of distress.

Jean Carmelo had drunk a decent amount of water, but that was several hours ago. He kept his head on a swivel, staying on his feet for hours. Over the past three or four years, his body had become accustomed to occasional fasts. That enabled him to unconsciously suspend his urges to excrete waste. He was in fight mode, unwilling to get caught in a compromising position. By keeping his eyes open, he was able to concentrate on solutions.

Throughout the night, residents, alone and confused, walked by and joined them. Others parked their vehicles on the road next to them, reclined their seats back, and tried to rest or fall asleep. They vented their grief and anger through religious quotes, prayer, and song. They cried and lamented being unable to get in contact with loved ones. Haiti's motto, L'Union Fait La Force" *Unity Creates Strength*, was rarely practiced by its inhabitants. It had become too common for minor disagreements to divide people. But disaster had turned strangers into friends, at least for the moment.

EXODUS

Jean Carmelo was realizing how much influence the media had on him. He replayed images of hurricane Katrina that had been seared into his consciousness: victims floating in the flood waters, damaged homes that had not been rebuilt, powerless families stranded on roofs. *Did anyone know what had happened in Port-au-Prince? Did anyone care?*

What about dad, Emmanuel, Anel, and Lauren? Was Grandma's house strong enough to withstand these quakes? Did dad get knocked to the ground? He was always so afraid of falling. Would anyone with him be able to help get him to safety? Is the puppy safe? His brain was full of questions, and being unable to get answers was becoming increasingly frustrating.

They all turned their attention to a sudden rush of commotion all around them. Moving vehicles were increasing in number and traveling more erratically. Screaming women with children and men with tears of horror running down their cheeks sprinted past them. They were all heading in the same direction. Some led the way with flashlights. Others carried kerosene lamps.

Dominique asked a middle-aged woman, her hair in rollers, "Pou ki sa tout moun pe kou nyé-a?" *Why is everyone so scared all of a sudden?*

"Gin yin yon sounami kap vini! Tou t moun anba mòn nan di yo tande d-lo!" *There's a tsunami coming our way! The people at the bottom of the mountain said they heard water!* she said before disappearing in a flash.

Jean Carmelo figured someone may have heard the word on the radio and jumped to conclusions. Others coming up the mountain claimed that a volcano close by was on the verge of erupting.

A man holding a portable radio and a flashlight yelled, "Fo nou tou-t monté pi-wo ké nou ka rivé." *We must go as high as we can!*

One thing was clear: adversity had once again recognized the Haitian people as worthy opponents. Not wanting to take any chances, Jean Carmelo and his group looked at each other and decided to find safer haven up the mountain.

It was past nine-thirty p.m. Dominique's Isuzu Trooper would have to fit six or seven people. Rose was unsure what to do. Jean Carmelo grabbed her hand and decided that they should start walking while Dominique got his car ready. It was a toss-up as to which method was safer, but he had to get his mother moving to a higher elevation as quickly as possible.

They walked sprightly through the rocky, holey streets. Rose gripped his hand firmly, focusing on maintaining her footing. They made sure to lift their feet high with each step. It was dark so they had to avoid tripping over the large rocks and debris on the road. Ten minutes later, they came to a wall blocking the street. They now had to make a decision to go right or left.

Rose tugged on his arm. "We should wait for Dominique to come with his jeep."

Jean Carmelo directed her off the street, and they positioned themselves with their backs against the wall, looking at the swarm of headlights and wide-eyed residents.

"Is that them?" Rose squinted at an approaching SUV.

Jean Carmelo knew the shapes of automobiles well enough to know that the SUV wasn't boxy enough. "No, that's not it, Ma."

They were standing in the middle of chaos, not knowing the landscape in the daytime, let alone in the darkness and during a crisis. Another vehicle's headlights approached them.

"There he is!" Rose yelled as she pulled Jean Carmelo's arm.

"That's not them, Mom. Relax! We'll get out of this. Just take it easy and breathe!" he assured her.

They waited. Jean Carmelo had no clue how they were going to get out of that mess. *Straying off into the unknown with no communication was not such a great move. Okay, breathe, kiddo. Just breathe and pay attention. What we're looking for is searching for us too.*

The crowds were remarkably civil and orderly. Despite the emotions they all were going through, there was no pushing or shoving. Younger people assisted older, less physically able individuals. The humanity inside of them realized that they needed to be united and strong. The next set of headlights appeared familiar to Jean Carmelo. He was confident it was the Trooper.

"Let's go, Mom. There he is!" He pulled her forward.

They walked over to the driver's side window.

Dominique rolled down his window. "Where are you going?"

"We're trying to get to a higher position on this mountain," Jean Carmelo replied.

"Come on, get in!"

The jeep was packed. Emmanuel was sitting in the passenger seat and got out to make room for Rose. There were no other seats available. Jean

Carmelo told Dominique to open the hatch door. A spare tire and Renee's walker lay flat behind the back row of seats. It was cramped, but Jean Carmelo was the only one flexible enough to sit there. He got in, and Dominique shut the door.

"Where is the rest of the group?" Jean Carmelo asked.

The response was drowned out by the loud horn behind them. Jean Carmelo heard enough to gather that some of the members of their group had decided to stay behind. They didn't buy the talk of tsunamis or volcano eruptions.

It was going to be one agonizing ride. Jean Carmelo focused on helping Dominique navigate by being his eyes in the back of the jeep. Jean Carmelo sat on the dusty spare tire with one foot on the rear door and his other leg bent under him. Other than going up the steep, rutted mountain, they didn't know where they were going. The jeep had no radio, and they'd left the small radio back with the rest of the group. Many of the roads were blocked off with the makeshift tents of those who had lost their homes.

They came upon a large group of people who had just watched their homes collapse and families die. Using chairs, beds, stoves, lamps, and the rest of their remaining belongings, they had blocked off the road. Dead bodies were lying in the street, and they didn't want anyone to step or run over them.

Making a U-turn on those narrow roads on a bicycle would have been a challenge. Jean Carmelo suggested that Dominique back up slowly and perform three-point turns. Each time they had to change direction, it was a chore. Not only did the tires constantly get stuck in holes Jean Carmelo couldn't see, but so many people were trying to get around the jeep. Jean Carmelo was not able to help as much as he wanted to, but he felt they were making the best decisions under the circumstances.

Seconds later, they felt another aftershock. The crowd screamed and felt a jolt of urgency to get higher. Even in their frightened state, pedestrians offered their help in making sure the jeep didn't hit anything or hurt anyone.

"Fè bak! Ou mèt Alé!"- *Move back! You can keep going!* They yelled.

They reached a point where they couldn't drive any farther. Foot travel was the only way up to the remote areas. They figured that they had covered a good enough distance, and found a temporary place to park. Dominique stepped out and walked off to urinate on a wall. Jean Carmelo took the opportunity to stretch while the others remained in the jeep. He had been rolled up and bouncing around while concentrating on not bashing his head against the vehicle's hard interior. That was becoming a habit with him during the trip.

Once he got out the jeep, he didn't smell water. Port-au-Prince was right off the water, and he pictured a map in his head of where they were. More people in Haiti either lived on or near higher ground. Jean Carmelo couldn't picture water coming up high enough to drown them all. Then again, he could never fathom what they were enduring.

* * * *

After a couple of painfully nervous hours, waiting for the unfathomable to occur, they decided to head down toward the house to rejoin the rest of the group. They got back in the Trooper and made their way back down the mountain, pushing through the massive migration still trekking up the hill. Dominique asked people along the way what roads were blocked.

They finally found their way back to the others. They were seated in the middle of the street, huddled under blankets. The temperature had been close to ninety degrees that afternoon; it had since dropped into the forties. A woman and a young adolescent girl dressed in her school uniform came running over to the group. It was Rose's sister Rochelle and her eleven-year-old daughter, Gege.

"We are so happy to see you! You're with family now," Rose said, embracing them.

By that point, the aftershocks had continued throughout the night at a rate of about one or two per hour. Jean Carmelo, Rose, and Emmanuel exchanged stories about what they saw during their brief split. The brave among them went inside to retrieve bread, water, and more blankets. They passed some hard dough bread around. As a group, they were somber and exhausted. The violent, unpredictable forces had taken a toll on all of them. Sitting in darkness hour after hour had become increasingly wearisome.

Gege and Jacob were shaken. They leaned on each other's shoulders, shivering until they fell asleep in uncomfortable positions. Jean Carmelo's body was becoming cold and stiff. The connection between the heart and the mind was vital in maintaining composure and focusing on keeping warm. He walked around, shaking out his arms and legs to summon some blood flow to his extremities.

In less than two hours, the sun would rise, and they would be able to say that they had made it through the night. Jean Carmelo had never been so anxious to see the sun. It meant light, warmth, life, spiritual energy, comfort, and endless possibilities. If some giant tidal wave were to take him and his family out, he wanted to see it coming.

A bright group of stars hung over them. The sky seemed to literally be falling. *I never understood that expression as a kid. The sky feels incredibly close, and as amazing as it is, it just doesn't feel comfortable. I don't know if this will be our last night, but we are sitting ducks right now.*

It was like being in a planetarium. He remembered that the constellation of Andromeda was millions of light-years away from Earth but still visible to the naked eye. The stars above had seemed to change positions in the sky. He couldn't locate stars that he had spotted minutes earlier. *Were they were really changing patterns? Was it fatigue and hallucinations from the shock that was starting to set in.?*

The radio was on, and the projected death totals from doctors and clergymen kept increasing. Word came through the speakers that the national penitentiary had collapsed. Thousands of prisoners had escaped. That could prove to be justice for many. Prisoners were frequently held indefinitely without ever being charged or receiving a fair trial. The best news of the night had to be when the radio said that the tsunami warning had been lifted.

Jean Carmelo walked over to open the rear passenger side door of the jeep. He climbed in and sat next to Emmanuel, who stared ahead, tight-lipped. Jean Carmelo's teeth chattered as his body shook. Covered from head to toe in goose bumps, he shivered with his arms folded underneath his T-shirt. Attempting to achieve a modicum of comfort, he closed his strained eyes and leaned his head back as far as it could go without overstraining.

Another aftershock shook them. That one echoed far into the distance. He noticed that those on the chairs in front of the jeep gave a little more of a reaction. The four tires in the jeep appeared to cushion the sensation to a degree. Howling and squeals of fear and pain from the dog across the street continued throughout the night.

Rays of Uncertainty

A bright orange glow peeked out from behind the white clouds. It had been a good two hours since the last tremor. Jean Carmelo knew that it was just the beginning though. If they could make it through an earthquake, then what couldn't they make it through? Once each individual overcame his personal purgatories, maybe they could use that tragedy as a trampoline to reach new heights. Whatever the future held, the sun would be above them as a visual and spiritual guide.

As the sun continued to make its ascent, Jean Carmelo observed the temperature and the prospects for a better day increase. The birds made their way back to the rooftops. Cats came out from where they had been hidden throughout the night.

Phone service was still out. Everyone was anxious to know how loved ones were doing. Dominique and Jean Carmelo checked the house for damage. There were cracks on the exterior next to the front door. Longer cracks stretched from the ceiling to the upper portion of the wall. No one else dared to enter the house.

Jean Carmelo couldn't stop thinking about his dad. He gathered everyone willing to take the trip to his grandmother's house. Rose and Emmanuel sat in the rear seat while Jean Carmelo sat shotgun. It was their first opportunity to see the affliction done to the surrounding areas.

The ride was the most emotionally challenging trip any of them had ever taken. It was nothing short of horrific. Dozens of homes and small businesses had collapsed and been reduced to rubble. A young, relatively fit young man and his adolescent son stood behind a tall pile of cinder blocks. They were hysterical, digging for lost loved ones believed to be buried. It was one of countless similar scenes.

Before that day, Port-au-Prince had been more or less in a state of bedlam. No word could describe what they saw. Stunned survivors with cuts and bloody bruises roamed the streets, searching for food, water, fuel, and places to settle. Piles of stinky trash lined the sides of the roads. Crushed limbs and decaying bodies lay under and stuck out from the piles of debris. Residents shook their heads, crying and assessing the wreckage. Underneath the morning sun, people walked and prayed and gave updates on what major buildings had been destroyed.

"Katedral la se pa plis!" *The cathedral is no more!* one wiry, wide-eyed man yelled.

"Cathédrale de Port-au-Prince?" Rose asked, alarmed and shocked.

"Wi, li tonbe. Archbishop Miot mouri!" *Yes, it fell. Archbishop Miot has died!* he said with tears streaming down his face.

"That was where I had my first communion!" Rose said.

They drove off, continuing to observe the street. Every vendor with water or food was mobbed by large crowds pleading to get the last of whatever they had.

Less than one block from Rose's mother's house, a peculiar commotion captured everyone's attention. Dominique pulled over, and everyone got out of the jeep. They followed the people in front of them. The anguish and tears on each face suggested that something grave had happened that they probably didn't want to see it.

Hundreds of people were gathered around the College Catherine Flon School. Large sections of the school's structure had weakened and given way while afternoon classes were in session. Dozens of desks and chairs were visible from outside the building. Three classrooms were exposed after the concrete walls and floors had crumbled, sending teachers and students to their deaths. Friends and family of students wore T-shirts and handkerchiefs tied around their mouths and noses to withstand the stench.

Adolescent and adult men stood on hills of concrete rubble, forming human chains. The crowd grew thicker as word spread around town. Many of the five thousand children who had attended the school did not escape. The men passed inanimate victims slowly down the line.

A teenaged boy emerged from the crowd. He was bleeding profusely from a gash near his left ear. Praying loudly, he exclaimed, "Sè mwen! Mwen pa ka jwenn sè m'!" *My sister! I can't find my sister!* Clenching his teeth, he pointed toward a towering pile of debris as if he had last seen her there.

He lost his balance, falling into the arms of a middle-aged man and woman standing behind him. They slowly placed him on the ground. The woman signaled to those around her by raising her arm.

She yelled, "Atansyon!" *Watch out!* She raised her voice to warn the oncoming crowd to avoid stomping on the boy. "Mwen bezwen yon bagay pou blese sa a!" *I need something for this cut!*

The man beside her helped to calm the boy down. He removed his T-shirt and tied it around the boy's sweat-drenched head to staunch the blood flow. It was just one of numerous times strangers came together to find a solution.

Jean Carmelo couldn't imagine so many bystanders being so close to a scene that gruesome back in the United States. Law enforcement officials would have blocked off streets with yellow tape, and the scene would have been crawling with paramedics and authority figures. There was no such thing in Port-au-Prince. There were no police in sight. There wasn't even any hope that an ambulance would arrive soon.

Dominique and Rose were a few paces ahead of Jean Carmelo and Emmanuel. When they finally got through the crowd, they saw the base of a pyramid of neatly stacked, lifeless young men and women. The pile grew taller by the minute. Thin rivers of blood oozed from their mouths, noses, ears, and eye sockets. A powerful stench blew into their nostrils. Jean Carmelo took a second to look into as many faces as he could without breaking down. Some appeared to be in agony while others seemed peaceful. One boy was placed gently on his back by two men. His left eyelid twitched slowly before his final moments.

A chill ran through Jean Carmelo as he pulled out his camera. He knew right then and there that remaining sane would be an ongoing challenge. He took some shots of the scene but was cautious about taking pictures of bodies. He knew that once he focused on what he was shooting, he would not only lose the extraordinary rush of sensory details through the lens of the camera, but he would have to revisit that memory. That moment would remain tattooed on his hippocampus for the rest of his life.

Kids from kindergarten to twelfth grade had been making great efforts to take advantage of the fortune granted to them as students. Haitian families place an enormous emphasis on learning, but about half the adult population was illiterate. Without an education, their chances of securing any of the scarce work available were limited. Some low- and middle-income families sacrificed all they had to send their kids to school. Most schools were private, which meant uniforms and costly tuition. The lack of qualified teachers was another obstacle for students looking to pass college entrance exams. College Catherine Flon had a long reputation for producing responsible kids who would later contribute to improving their neighborhoods. It was devastating to see so many bright future prospects take such monumental steps back.

Jean Carmelo looked around and realized that the only person near him who he recognized was Emmanuel. Jean Carmelo had lost sight of Dominique and Rose. The crowd was increasing exponentially as news of the horrendous tragedy spread. The malodor in the air was overwhelming. Jean Carmelo was stunned and anxious. He grabbed Emmanuel and asked if he had seen the others.

Gesturing toward a spot in the distance, he said, "Yo te la!" *They were there!*

They decided to walk around the corner to Jean Carmelo's grandmother's house, anticipating they would find the others there. Along the way, they several street merchants had set up shop underneath makeshift tents. The price of bread, water, cooking oil, rice, beans, and charcoal had more than doubled. Mobs formed around anyone who had resources. Vendors fielded arguments from customers who were attempting to bargain down prices.

Emmanuel and Jean Carmelo walked up to the front gate. Anel and Lauren were there to welcome them in. They greeted each other with hugs. Jean Carmelo felt so good to see familiar faces again, even if it had only been a day and a half since they had last seen each other. Rose and Dominique stood inside talking with Jules, who was sitting in a wooden rocking chair on the patio.

Jean Carmelo walked over and gave him a hug, relieved that his father had no noticeable injuries. "Dad, where were you when the shaking started?"

"I think I was in the bedroom... sleeping," Jules said.

"What did you do next?"

"Nothing. What could I do?"

Much like everyone else, he hadn't realized what was going on. It didn't seem as if he'd made much effort to escape the house. Jean Carmelo was content with the fact that they were all alive. They talked about what they had seen at the school.

"When I heard the loud crash, I did not know what it was. I checked out the damage before you came. I knew a few kids who were scheduled to graduate this year," Anel said, shaking his head.

Jean Carmelo walked around the house to check for any signs of destruction. The outhouse had had a weak foundation, so it was no surprise that it had crumbled. The adult dogs were barely responsive to Jean Carmelo's presence. The puppy came running as fast as his little legs could move. He jumped onto Jean Carmelo's sneakers, bouncing with joy as his brown eyes reflected sunlight. Jean Carmelo crouched in front of the pup, petting him while he playfully nibbled at his fingers. Jean Carmelo was just as happy to see him unharmed. He picked up the puppy to see if he was hurt at all, but he seemed just fine.

When Jean Carmelo put him down for slap boxing, the puppy playfully attacked Jean Carmelo with the same energy and agility. That's when Jean Carmelo decided to call him Chamberlain. The name meant "chief officer of the household".

Jean Carmelo noticed that the tin shed in the backyard had also fallen down. The tall concrete wall that separated the yard from the street had crumbled almost completely. On the street, dozens of men, women, and children camped out on lounge chairs underneath umbrellas.

Dominique was leaving to see if he could get news of other family and friends in the area. He said that he would return tomorrow. Jules was still sitting in the patio, so Jean Carmelo pulled another chair over and sat down next to him. They watched as Chamberlain's mother, her coat revealing every last one of her ribs, gingerly walked by the white gate they were seated behind.

Jules turned to Jean Carmelo. "That's no good!" He called Anel, who was standing behind the front gate next to the street. "Why aren't the dogs fed?"

"She doesn't want to be nourished."

"As long as I'm here, I want you to make sure that the dogs get enough to eat! Do you understand?" Jules demanded.

"Qui." Anel answered, looking at Jean Carmelo with a confused expression.

Jules must not have realized that it would become a challenge for any of them to get food. Many vendors were dead or buried under rubble.

Crowds of irate men and women were getting extremely loud and rowdy. Scavengers with machetes, knives, and guns were running around collecting money, jewelry, and any possessions of value from dead bodies. Family and friends of the victims became outraged and decided to implement their own justice. A number of brave individuals offered to defend the bodies.

One of the suspected violators, a reedy-bodied man in his late thirties, tried to run away from the vigilantes. He tripped in the street and stumbled onto one knee. Several middle-aged men and women with large rocks and bottles surrounded him. He was old enough to know right from wrong, and he was found to be guilty in the court of public opinion.

He slowly got to his feet and feinted an attack at a young man with his dull, rusty machete. The young man stood in a defensive fighting stance with the weight of his body evenly distributed on the balls of his feet. He bobbed and weaved, slipping under the blade, and tackled the scavenger to the ground. Two other men jumped in and quickly relieved the violator of his weapon. They dug through his pants pockets and retrieved driver's licenses, jewelry, pictures, cell phones, and loose cash. The man was kicked and beaten in an alleyway between two apartments. He was allowed to limp away, but Jean Carmelo didn't know if he would survive his injuries.

The hospitals that had been operating before the earthquake were severely understaffed and barely equipped to handle the needs of the city. Now, just like other buildings, they had been reduced to rubble. Qualified medical personnel were nowhere to be found. Many of them had died or were in need of medical attention themselves.

Morgues filled beyond capacity, and people scrambled to find caskets and open places to bury the dead. Others would find scraps of metal to sell or save whatever they could. Only a few could afford proper burials. That was crushing, because providing a proper burial allowed families to witness an individual's spirit leave the body in a dignified manner. People without much money would save for years to be buried in a decent casket with meaningful ceremonies.

Jean Carmelo's grandmother's funeral had been scheduled to take place in a few days, but there was still no telephone communication. No one knew if the priest and his clergy were alive or if the funeral parlor was still standing. Even if they could reach him, there was no guarantee the ceremony could happen. Haiti's already fragile infrastructure had collapsed entirely, and there were no alternate routes to relief. The country had only two international airports, one in Cap-Haïtien and the other in Port-au-Prince, leaving the capital as the primary gateway for foreign aid. But Port-au-Prince, the center of power and resources, was itself in ruins. Supplies trickled in painfully slowly. With roads blocked by debris and no reliable transportation network, getting help beyond the capital was nearly impossible.

Jean Carmelo had been awake since early Tuesday morning, and he felt every inch of his body becoming rigid from the stress. He tried to channel the muscle memory that wouldn't allow him to quit when he was hitting the punching bag or sprinting on the track. But it was no use. His body's energy supply was nearing exhaustion. He could no longer think or see clearly.

Jules and Rose sat at the dining room table, talking, resting, and thinking while sipping cups of tea. Jean Carmelo wasn't hungry but agreed to drink some tea before he crashed. Rose passed him a white ceramic cup and poured in hot tea from a silver kettle. Jean Carmelo motioned her to stop pouring when the cup got close to full. It was very warm but not hot enough to burn his mouth, so he swallowed it in one big gulp as if it were medicine.

He wobbled over to the sofa and dropped himself on the thick, plastic-covered cushions. The second he put his head down, he felt his ears ringing and a buzz coming from the ground. He knew he wouldn't sleep for long under those conditions. The threat of being in or around collapsing buildings remained ominous. Falling asleep when the sun was out had never been easy for him, but a few hours would enable Jean Carmelo to think and function on recharged batteries.

SUPPLY AND DEMAND

Jean Carmelo opened his eyes three hours later, concerned that he couldn't feel the ground under his feet. He looked around and noticed his feet were elevated, and he was lying down with his face stuck to the warm plastic covering the sofa. Jules was still sitting at one end of the dining room table. Wiping drool from his mouth, Jean Carmelo heard Rose and Emmanuel talking in one of the bedrooms. He felt as if time had stood still while his eyes were shut. Tension blurred his vision as he slowly got up in a daze.

Anel stood in front of the gate entrance and placed a white metal sign with blue trim to hang from the gate. The heart-shaped sign was a recognizable symbol that let people passing by know that someone in the family had passed away.

By the front door, a portable AM/FM radio on the top shelf was on at a moderate volume. Two voices gave words of encouragement and discussed updated death tolls and other developments. Jean Carmelo was dumbstruck as to why he had not heard anyone from the presidential palace giving announcements or suggesting any courses of action. He wondered if they were still alive...

Loud roars erupted from the crowds outside. Another aftershock trekked through the city like a great white shark searching for prey. Getting comfortable for any amount of time was impossible. Jean Carmelo felt dehydrated, and he got up to serve himself a glass of Culligan water from the last five-gallon bottle left. They didn't have enough to last them the rest of the day, and it was anyone's guess as to where they would get more.

Drinking tap water was out of the question. The water that flowed through the pipes probably contained bacteria that scientists probably hadn't named yet. Rose was the only one among them with any Haitian money. Jean Carmelo had a hundred American dollars on him. Unfortunately, vendors didn't favor American money because it was too much trouble for them to convert. Only hustlers and airport employees did business with it.

Rose walked toward Jean Carmelo. "How did you sleep, son?"

"Not too good. I'm still tired." He sat up with his hand clasped over his head, still in a daze.

"Why don't you go back to sleep?"

"You know I can't sleep much in the daytime."

"Even though you stayed up all night? You need rest!" She pleaded.

Howling and growling from the dogs preceded the sound of knuckles knocking on the front gate. Two teenaged girls waited to come in. When Jean Carmelo walked over to see what they wanted, they said they'd known his grandmother and wanted to give their condolences.

"Je m'appelle Celine. Ca c'est ma soeur Alice," *My name is Celine. This is my sister Alice,* Celine, the older of the two, said.

"Bonsoir," Alice said.

"Bonsoir. Je m'appelle Jean Carmelo." *Hello. My name is Jean Carmelo.* They shook hands. He motioned for them to follow him into the house. "Asseyez-vous s'il vous plaît." *Please sit down.* He pointed at the chairs in the living room.

Rose walked in from the back of the house with Lauren.

"Vous voulez de l'eau?" *Do you want some water?* Rose asked.

"Oui s'il vous plait," *Yes please,* they replied.

Celine wore her hair in braids that came down to her shoulders. Alice had shiny, black curls. Lauren came back with a plastic pitcher, two glasses, and a couple of napkins on a tray. Rose and Jean Carmelo sat down. The two girls sat across from them.

"Où étais-tu hier après-midi?" *Where were you yesterday afternoon?* Rose asked.

They described how they were supposed to have been in nursing school at the time of the earthquake.

"Alice bliye youn nan liv li. Li te gen yon pwojè akòz, se konsa li tounen al jwenn li." - *Alice forgot one of her books. She had a project due, so she went back to get it.* Celine said, tears welling up in her eyes.

"Lè nou te mache tounen ak te rive nan bor yo nan pwopriyete lekòl la, yon gwo fòs soti nan anba tè a jete nou desann," *When we walked back and got to the edges of the school property, a powerful force from underneath the ground threw us down,* Alice said.

"Nou pa t 'konnen ki sa fè!" *We didn't know what to do!* Celine cried.

With tears glistening in their eyes, they both moved to sit between Rose and Jean Carmelo on the couch. Rose stroked Alice's long, black hair. Celine tried to describe staying on the ground and hearing their classmates scream and suffer during their final moments.

"Te nou ale nan klas, nou ta te peri tou!" *Had we gone to class, we would have perished too!* Celine said.

"La journée d'hier a été triste pour nous tous mais Dieu nous donne toujours la force!" *Yesterday was a sad day for all of us but our God will always give us strength,* Rose said.

Jean Carmelo put his arms around Celine's shoulders. "We will make it through this."

The music coming from the radio was interrupted by a voice. The DJ announced that over a hundred schools were confirmed collapsed or damaged in the Port-au-Prince area. Thousands of children were still buried underneath rubble. The future of the country had already been in limbo. Now, many were left wondering where hope would come from. Decades earlier, Dr. François "Papa Doc" Duvalier, proclaimed dictatorship over the country. Young intellectuals became fearful over the shift of power and government policy. Professors, medical doctors and social scientists fled to other countries. They went on to play major roles in developing the education systems, hospitals, and agricultural organizations of Canada, Senegal, Cameroon, Ghana, Chad and other countries. The shortage of qualified professionals was staggering before. Now, those who were left were either dead or fighting for their own survival.

Celine surveyed the living room and dining room and gave Alice a puzzled expression.

" Ki sa ki nan mal?" *What's wrong?* Alice asked.

"Li santi l konsa etranj yo chita isit la epi yo pa wè zanmi nou an." *It feels so strange to sit here and not see our friend,* Celine said.

"Wi, manman m 'kite nou kèk semèn de sa. Lè m 'te vizite l' dènyèman, li te di m 'ke lide mande l' ansanm ak tout kò yo te fatige. Li ta di nenpòt ki moun ki t 'vle koute ke li te bezwen repo. Sou jou a mwen te kite, li te di m 'ki tan kap vini an ta dwe trè difisil pou nou e ke li te nan

ase." *Yes, my mother left us some weeks ago. When I visited her recently, she told me that her mind and body were tired. She would tell anyone who would listen that she needed rest. On the day I left, she told me that the future would be very tough for us and that she had been through enough,* Rose said.

"Petèt li te santi sa ki te vini?" *Maybe she felt what was coming?"* Alice said.

"Mwen panse ke li ka gen li te ye yon bagay." *I think she may have known something,* Rose concurred.

"Apre lekòl, nou ta vin isit la tout tan tout tan an kenbe konpayi li." *After school, we would come here all the time to keep her company,* Celine said. "She would always have a story for us and tell us about how things were when she was growing up."

"Te grann nou te mouri nan malarya anvan nou te resevwa yon chans konnen l'." *Our grandmother had died from malaria before we got a chance to know her,* Alice said.

"Manman ou te anseye nou anpil bagay sou ki jan yo pote tèt nou kòm ti fi, ak sa vle di tèlman yo nou." *Your mother taught us a lot about how to carry ourselves as girls, and that meant so much to us,* Celine said.

Listening to those girls reminisce gave Jean Carmelo another perspective of how much his grandmother meant to those around her. Her influence in the lives of the girls said a great deal about the effect extended families had in the development of children into young adults.

Two lanky young men appeared at the front gate. They announced their presence, "Onè." *Honor.*

Jules responded, "Respè." *Respect.*

The taller and thinner of the two introduced himself as Rudy. The other said his name was Paul. They had come to pick up Rose and take her to find out if one of her friends was okay.

"Ou pral oblije eskize m ', ti fi mwen an" *You'll have to excuse me, girls*, Rose said. "Mwen gen kèk moun isit la yo pran m 'lòt bò lanmè a nan lavil la. Ou ap akeyi yo rete si ou ta renmen." *I have some people here to take me to the other side of town. You're welcome to stay if you'd like.*

"Nou ka tounen pita." *We can come back later*, Alice said.

"Ou gen yon moun yo rete ak nan kay la?" *Do you have someone to stay with at home?* Rose asked.

"Wi, bòpè nou an se lakay kounye a." *Yes, our stepfather is home right now, Celine* said.

"Oke, di ou mèsi pou kanpe pa." *Okay, thank you for stopping by*, Rose said.

"Babay." *Good-bye.* The girls waved as they left.

Rose invited Paul and Rudy inside. "Ou ka gen yon chèz. Mwen pral jis yon kèk minit pi long lan." *You can have a seat. I'll be just a few minutes longer.*

"Pran tan ou. Nou pral pale ak jeneral la." *Take your time. We'll talk with the general.* Rudy laughed.

They walked over to see Jules, who was sitting on the patio listening to the radio. They shook hands and waved to everyone inside before sitting with Jules.

Rudy told Jules what he had been doing moments before the first tremor. "Mwen te nan estasyon gaz la ap resevwa kèk gaz pou machin mwen an, lè tout nan yon toudenkou, mwen te santi tè a souke ak Tonben. Mwen te panse ke nou te frape pa yon meteor!" *I was at the gas station getting some gas for my car when all of a sudden, I felt the earth shaking and crumbling. I thought that we had been hit by a meteor!*

"Enkwayab!" *Unbelievable!* Jules said.

"Jou pi bonè, mwen te lekti sou etranje ak ki jan nou pa ta ka fòm yo sèlman nan lavi sou planèt sa a oswa nan linivè la. Mwen te panse ki te petèt yon bato espas te ateri!" *Days earlier, I had been reading about aliens and how we might not be the only forms of life on this planet or in the universe. I was thinking that maybe a spaceship had landed!* Rudy continued.

"Lavi ya terib," *Life is terrible,* Jules said, shaking his head.

"Lè Mwen te kondwi ale tounen lakay, mwen te wè yo te lakay mwen detwi nèt!" *When I drove back home, I saw my house was completely destroyed!* Rudy said.

"Èske moun mouri?" *Did anyone die?* Jules asked.

"Non, gras a dye okenn moun pa mouri," *No, by the grace of God nobody died,* Rudy replied.

Jules looked at Rudy and appeared as if he had something to say. Instead, he asked again, "Èske moun mouri?"

Rudy and Paul looked at each other to confirm that they heard him correctly.

"Non, okenn moun pas mouri," *No, no one died,* Paul replied, grinning as he spoke his first words since they'd arrived.

Rose came out to greet the two men and told them that all she had to offer was their remaining water. They said that they were fine.

Jean Carmelo heard them getting ready to leave and said he wanted to tag along. He was protective around his parents, even more so than before they arrived. He wanted to account for them at all times. It tore at him to not stay with Jules, and it frustrated him that his father was putting forth less effort to move. He'd noticed the confusion on Lauren and Anel's faces when Jules called for them. They came to see what he wanted, and it was always to ask them to do something he was capable of doing himself.

The four of them walked out to a white Toyota pickup truck. Jean Carmelo helped his mom into the passenger seat, and Rudy got behind the wheel. Paul and Jean Carmelo hopped into the back of the truck. Standing in the bed gave Jean Carmelo a view over the hundreds of people lining the streets, focused on their missions. Men stood off to the side of the road, urinating on rocks and trash. Women bent down to pick up bits of food from the ground. Many walked as couples or groups. Rudy came to a stop to avoid a pothole in the middle of the road.

An elderly man walking with a cane asked, "Ou ka ban mwen woulib? Pie m fè m mal. Mwen pa kabap mache pilwen." *Can you give me a ride? My foot hurts. I don't think I can walk any further.*

"Ban m 'men ou," *Give me your hand,* Jean Carmelo said, extending his hand.

"Merci," the man replied.

Jean Carmelo helped him up and leaned him against the cab wall. "Mete pyé ou sou sa." *Here put your foot on this.* Jean Carmelo placed a black milk crate under the man's severely wounded left foot. "Kouman sa rive?" *How did that happen?*

"Yon gro ròch sot tonbé sou li lè mwen tap eseyé kouri." *A big rock fell on it as I was trying to run away.*

"Kote li soti?" *Where did it come from?* Paul asked.

"Li sorti nan twa kay la," *It fell from the rooftop,* the man replied.

"Èske tout moun sove?" *Did everyone make it out?* Jean Carmelo asked.

"Non, madanm mwen mouri." *No, my wife is dead.*

"Eskize m," *I'm sorry,* Jean Carmelo replied.

Jean Carmelo pulled out his handheld digital camera and took pictures of the surrounding area. Two armed Haitian police officers rode in the back of a marked pickup truck. For the most part, their presence was low-key. They seemed to be concerned with their own safety, observing and keeping their interactions with the people to a minimum. Every third or fourth building had sustained some type of structural damage.

Once they turned onto the side streets, the damage became much more evident. One house had an entire bedroom and portions of the ceiling collapse onto the street. Homes had been completely flattened, some with the residents still in them. The owners who were still alive sat in chairs with those who had lost everything. Walls on both sides of many of the back roads spilled into the middle, making those streets off-limits to vehicles. Tent encampments had sprouted all throughout the city.

"Rete la souple!" *Stop here please!* the elderly man said.

Rudy stopped, and Jean Carmelo and Paul helped him out of the truck.

"Merci," the man said.

"Kenbe kò ou," *Take care,* they replied.

Rudy continued to drive along a water source outlined with moderate-sized stone, clay, concrete houses, and trees. They came to a steep descent which led to the bottom of a rocky river. Defenseless kids with handsome smiles continued to persevere without any signs of suffering on their faces. They used small buckets to wash themselves outside.

Women and young girls balanced buckets on their heads. Men and boys carried plastic buckets of water. They walked across a narrow bridge extending from one side of the river to the other. The metal railings on each side were painted the colors of the Haitian flag. Below them, the brown water was saturated with garbage and hazardous waste. Goats and fat, furry black pigs rummaged through the dump.

Rudy drove toward the shallowest section of murky water. The driver of a small jeep heading in the opposite direction was halfway under water and needed a push to get across. Jean Carmelo and Paul hung onto the metal rails on the back of the truck while Rudy peeled out on some rocks below the surface of the water. They began moving up the steep hill. The higher they climbed, the more the terrain leveled out.

* * * *

They arrived at Rochelle's house. She was standing out front shaking her head in disbelief. The tall, two-story home was badly damaged. Chunks of concrete were missing from the upper floor, and concrete masses were deposited on all sides of the house. They entered through a side gate entrance.

"Katastwof!" *Catastrophe!* Rochelle said, shaking her head.

Rochelle needed to get the dress she was planning to wear for the funeral. She was the only one who knew where it was, and no one felt comfortable letting her go inside alone. Once inside, the first thing they saw was the remnants of the kitchen. Dark gray concrete powder covered the sink, counter, and floor. Every wall had deep cracks and chipped paint with debris everywhere.

Fearing another aftershock would easily demolish what was left of the house, Jean Carmelo told everyone, "Let's get what we need and get out as soon as possible!"

As tempting as it was to stroll down memory lane, nowhere indoors was safe. Rochelle and her daughter would not have made it if they had been in their house on Tuesday. Rochelle found her dress in the closet where she'd left it. Luckily, it had been wrapped in plastic, so it was all white except for gray spots on the bottom hem.

* * * *

The last rays of the sun retreated into the dark blue sky. Although the aftershocks had been steady throughout the day, something about the lack of light created a sense of increased vulnerability. If an object were to fall on them, the dark would make it more difficult to see it coming.

Jean Carmelo made up his bed to retire for the night. The room was dimly lit by a small kerosene lamp on the dining room table. He lay down, lightly shutting his eyes. His ears picked up people talking on the streets as he took a few moments to recap everything he had experienced over the past several days.

This is what it's like to live poor in Haiti. To not know where the next meal is coming from is an uneasy existence. To live life expecting seemingly insurmountable obstacles can wear and tear on the mind and body. People here continue to move forward, even when it appears as if all is lost.

He was startled by a sudden whistling sound. The mosquitoes were bad enough, but the visitor sounded as though it was much bigger and faster. The open-air designs on the walls allowed for a variety of insects and tropical wildlife to enter, but the new creature had feet that tapped and slid on the tiles. Jean Carmelo reached for his cell phone to shine light in the direction of the sound he'd heard. It was 2:15 a.m., and the creature was eager to hide. He turned over on his back and stayed silent. He was tired but alert.

"Cllliiiiiiiinng!" A metal cup fell to the floor from the dining room table.

Jean Carmelo sprang up in the bed. His heart was beating rapidly, but he was calm. He saw a long, pink tail. A grey rat the size of a baseball jumped off one of the dining room chairs and ran into the corner. Jean Carmelo got out of bed and moved toward it. The concentration of the dead had been attracting all sorts of rodents and pests.

He had been afraid of mice ever since his childhood. Their eyes and teeth were uninviting, and they were known to carry disease. A sudden rush of adrenaline had him ready to smash the creature with his bare feet. As he inched closer, the rat stayed close to the wall and scurried into the back bedrooms. He chased it, but the rat escaped through a crack near the bottom of the back door.

He retreated to bed knowing that nighttime was his best possibility to get some rest. It was the only time vehicles weren't on the streets. He heard a few voices, a few arguments here and there, and the humming of an electric streetlamp powered by a generator. Tucking the sheet over his ears, he tried to shield himself from the mosquitoes. Somehow, the relentless pests still found a way to buzz loudly around his ears. Maybe they were trying to tell him something? Whatever it was, if it didn't involve sleep, he wasn't interested. Objects in the room rattled. The earth trembled...

Jean Carmelo jumped out of the bed again and went to open the front door. He tried to turn the doorknob and push the door, but it was locked. Not only was the top lock shut, but the deadbolt was locked. *Why is this door locked? What the hell is going on?* Seconds later, the shaking stopped. Rose came out the bedroom in her night gown. Emmanuel stood outside his room down the hall.

"Where's Dad?" Jean Carmelo asked.

"I'm here. I'm okay," Jules answered from behind the curtain separating the bedroom from the dining room.

"Who's responsible for locking this door?" Jean Carmelo demanded.

"We are okay now," Rose said.

"No, this is not okay. This door can't be locked. I'm not having it. We're either borderline crazy or really over-confident for even being inside right now. We're not going out like that. No way!"

Rose showed him where the key was—right above the door, behind the small radio—and unlocked the door.

"Ma, you locked the door?"

"Jean Carmelo, lower your voice." She motioned for him to step out to the patio.

"Who did this, Ma?"

"It had to be either Emmanuel or Anel."

"Why?"

"When my mother was here, it was their responsibility to make sure everything was closed at night."

"Understood, but why would they do that now? That doesn't make any sense," Jean Carmelo said.

"They locked the door for safety."

"How is it safe to have a building fall on your head?"

"I know you know about the Tonton Macoute, right?" she asked.

"Yeah, that military thug gang."

"For years, they went through neighborhoods at night, breaking through gates, beating people up, raping women, and killing anyone for money or politics. They came with guns and machetes. Anel and Emmanuel knew many people who were victims. It still haunts them. That's why they locked the door."

"I really don't mean to be insensitive, Ma, but you feel this earth shaking all around us? That is what I'm most concerned with right now," Jean Carmelo said.

"I know you're agitated—"

"I sleep right by that door. For me not to be able to open it is insane. I was going to kick the door down!"

"I'm going back to sleep. I don't know what else to tell you. Good night," Rose said.

The frequency of menacing aftershocks began to reduce as the night progressed. On the street, a few dozen men and women sang and chanted hymns. Their voices cut through the air, and they sounded as if they were right in the backyard. That was their way of grieving, uniting with other survivors, and releasing nervous energy to deter those who might wish to do them harm. Surrounded by the ghosts of family and friends they would never see again, they continued to sing.

The next morning, some distance away, large machinery could be heard approaching. Whatever it was, it made people in the street hurry out of its way. Several government dump trucks stormed down the street. Anel told Jean Carmelo that they were making trips from College Catherine Flon to large graves.

Dozens of families had set up makeshift tents and cots underneath umbrellas in the backyard since the wall was no longer there. Instinctively, the dogs knew to leave them alone and continued guarding the front of the property. The shady area in the front yard was ideal for protection from the unforgiving sun.

Fatigue and dehydration was wearing down Rose. She was feeling the effects of trying to adjust to an environment that would not return to the way it was before. She asked Anel and Jean Carmelo why so many people were in the yard. They looked at each other and said nothing. She shouted at the people, asking them to remove themselves and go elsewhere. They looked at her with blank stares.

Jean Carmelo said, "Mom! They have nowhere else to go!"

"Yeah, but they keep bringing more and more with them into the yard!" she replied.

"Mom, please go back inside. Go and get some rest," Jean Carmelo said.

"There's no time for rest. I still haven't spoken with anyone from the funeral parlor," Rose replied. As if she just realized what she had done, she paused for a second and turned to walk inside.

Jean Carmelo followed her inside. "Is there something wrong with you?"

"I'm not feeling well." She rubbed her head.

"What's wrong?"

"It may be the water. I boiled some water and drank it this morning."

"Ah, that has to be it. You've got to take it easy until we can find something bottled."

"I'll be okay. I'm just having some stomach pain and gas."

The lack of water purification in the country was always a wide open door for a variety of diseases. Jean Carmelo felt guilty, wondering why their lives were spared. *How did we come away untouched? What makes us so worthy?*

He was beginning to come to grips with possibly going several days without food. He figured that was what he had been training for. The strength of him and his family would surely be tested. They were no longer living; they were surviving.

Phone service was still an unfunny joke, but word on the street was that the individuals in charge of arranging and performing the funeral were alive. The church and the funeral parlor had suffered minor structural damage with no deaths. As for family members unaccounted for throughout the country...

Rochelle and Rose took to the busy streets and began their trek to the funeral parlor three miles east.

Jean Carmelo noticed them closing the front gate. "Ma! Where are you two going?"

"We have to see if this funeral can be taken care of," she said.

"It's dangerous out there. I'll go with you," He said.

A decent funeral was one of the most important events in Haitian culture. Having a special outfit for the service or a set of clothes that were never worn for any other occasion was essential. It was necessary for the spirit of the dead to have proper respect and closure to put everyone involved at peace.

Rose, Jean Carmelo, and Rochelle walked along the dusty, weather-beaten roads filled with broken glass. Women sat on low wooden chairs underneath makeshift tarps surrounded by baskets with vegetables for sale. With dull stainless-steel knives, they peeled the rotten portions off of fruit and vegetables. Using hand-sized cardboard cutouts, they swatted away mosquitoes and flies.

As a pedestrian, the roads were walk-at-your-own-risk. Heavy vehicle traffic sped up and down constantly. Young men and women sat on duct-taped seats, pedaling their bicycles with unbending desire. Cargo trucks filled with water attempted to station and distribute to people in need. Large, multi-colored buses held dozens of bags on their roofs. Inside, refugees packed in, looking to cross town for opportunities and resources. Amidst the warm, street dust, and the stench of death, people were focused on finding food, shelter, and loved ones.

Rose handed Jean Carmelo a white plastic bag. In it was the dress Rose had selected for her mother to be dressed in during the funeral and burial. Rose was accustomed to being in crowds like that. For years, she'd ridden the New York subways, commuting from Long Island to Brooklyn. She walked quickly with her head up and a focused, navigational outlook. Rochelle was noticeably uncomfortable around so many people. She kept her head down, looking to avoid the potholes and puddles of sewage. Jean Carmelo walked with Rochelle, knowing that he was tall enough to look over the crowd.

The three of them approached a roadblock, one of the many throughout the capital. Police and government workers in bright orange vests were moving the crowd away from the limp bodies in the street. Jean Carmelo approached a government worker in his mid-forties.

He asked Jean Carmelo, "Kibò ou prale?" *Where are you going?*

"Nou bezwen pasé paské no pralé nan yon antèman," *We want to pass because we have to go to a funeral,* Jean Carmelo said.

"M'regrèt sa. Min nou pa kapab ale la. Moun mouri la." *I'm sorry. You can't go through here. There are dead people here.*

"Kote nou pralé?" *Where are we going?* Rochelle asked.

"Fò nou ale isit-la-menm," *You have to go right there,* the worker said, pointing at the congested street on his right.

Despite the typically eager and ultra-aggressive nature of large mobs, order was maintained. Single-file lines going in each direction formed. Horns from cars blared. Drivers were getting horrible gas mileage from constant stop-and-go-nowhere traffic. As disorganized as the roads were, Rochelle said that she knew where the detour would take them. They walked up the narrow, inclined street. Jean Carmelo made sure Rose and Rochelle didn't get hit by vehicles passing by.

"Rose, a lari pwochen fè adwat," *Rose, at the next street make a right,* Rochelle said.

"Pi devan?" *Further down?* Rose asked.

"Wi," Rochelle replied.

As they turned onto the steep and narrow road, small shops, churches, and low concrete buildings lined the perimeter. Each street revealed more damage. Homes had been reduced to piles of rubble. Cars and trucks were flattened in garages, and trees were uprooted. Collapsed walls spilled into the road. Tent cities took up large sections of some streets and totally blocked off others. Men, women, and children asked anyone who would listen for food and water. The harsh heat was unforgiving with temperatures rising into the nineties.

When they arrived, a small crowd was gathered in front of the funeral parlor. A dark-skinned man wearing a navy-blue suit stood at the tall iron door. He fielded questions about loved ones who had either just been killed or had ceremonies already scheduled. Rose, Jean Carmelo, and Rochelle made their way to the front.

"Mwen ka édé ou?" *Can I help you?* he asked.

"Wi, mwen vlé fè antéré manman mwen," *Yes, I want to have the burial for my mother.* Rose answered.

"Ou te la deja?" *You were here already?* he asked.

"Mwen péyé depi semen dènyé," *I already paid since last week,* Rose said.

"Ki non manman w?" *What is your mother's name?*

"Li rélé Rachelle," *Her name is Rachelle,* Rose replied.

"Map rélé Mark pou ou." *I'll call Mark for you.*

Dressed in crisp business casuals and dark sunglasses, Mark, the director of funeral arrangements, greeted them at the door and invited them in. "Mwen kontan fe konesans ou." *I am happy to meet you.*

"Se youn plézi pou mwen tou," *It's a pleasure to meet you too,* Rose replied.

They stepped inside, and the stench of dead bodies hit them with a powerful gust, causing everyone to cover their noses. Mark noticed their collective looks of disgust and motioned them to the right. He opened the sliding glass door of the viewing room. Once inside, he asked them if they wanted the door shut, and they all nodded. The stench halted as soon as he did.

The viewing room was lined with rows of black chairs. A dozen ceiling fans remained still, unable to provide relief. Toward the front of the room was a low stage where the caskets were usually positioned during viewings. Small video cameras set up on tripods faced the stage. They sat down to discuss their plans.

Mark wiped his brow with a blue handkerchief and said, "Mwen regrete pou chalè a. Mwen konnen li la alèz, men si mwen louvri pòt la, pran sant lan ap ranpli sal sa a byen vit. " *I apologize for the heat. I know it's uncomfortable, but if I open the door, the smell will fill this room quickly.*

"Pa yon pwoblèm. Nou apresye ou pran tan nan pale avèk nou." *Not a problem. We appreciate you taking the time to speak with us*, Rose said.

A man in his early thirties entered the room. He introduced himself as the priest who would conduct the ceremony and offered his condolences. He explained that the ceremony would have to be pushed to Saturday. Another family was also scheduled to have a wake and burial on Saturday. Although the church had suffered minimal damage, he couldn't promise conducting anything indoors due to the uncertainty of aftershocks.

Jean Carmelo handed the plastic bag to Rose. She opened it and pulled out a long, white dress with embroidery. The style was reminiscent of the dresses her mother had sewed as a young seamstress. Rose pulled a pair of white pearl earrings and a CD of hymns sung in French from her purse. She explained to Mark the way her mother should be displayed and what songs to play. He promised to honor her requests and said he would also reimburse her for any services that were no longer offered due to the circumstances. A limo was set to pick up each family member on Saturday.

"Kote wou rete?" *Where do you live?* Mark asked.

"Laba a," *Over there.* Jean Carmelo answered, pointing in the direction from which they came.

"Èské ou mache la ansanm?" *Did you all walk here together?* Mark asked.

"Wi," *Yes,* Jean Carmelo answered.

"Li fè cho anpil. M ap jwenn un chofè pou Mennen nan machine." *It's very hot. I will find a driver to take you by car.*

"Mesi anpil!" *Thank you very much!* Rose said.

"N a wè Samdi," *I'll see you Saturday,* Mark replied.

A few minutes later, they made their way out the front door. Vendors braving the hot, humid air sold various goods. Rose and Rochelle walked over to see what was for sale.

"They have crackers and boxes of cereal. Do you want any cereal?" Rose said to Jean Carmelo.

"Yes," Jean Carmelo replied.

"I don't see any milk."

"I can use water, Ma," he said.

A gold, mid-nineties Toyota Land Cruiser waited with the engine running. The driver smiled and invited them inside.

"Ma, our ride is here," Jean Carmelo said, helping Rose and Rochelle with their purchases. He opened the rear door for Rose and Rochelle, and he took the front passenger seat.

The driver introduced himself as Pierre. He reassured them that they would be able to get through the crowded streets despite the ever-growing roadblocks and tent cities.

"Kijan ou santi?" *How do you feel?* Rose asked him, noticing his effort to remain cool.

"Pafwa mwen santi m pa byen men n ap degaje," *Sometimes I don't feel so well, but we'll get by,* he said.

"Ou gen kouraj," *You have courage,* Rose said.

"Anpil moun mwen konnen mouri men nou toujou la pou yon rezon." *A lot of people I know are dead, but we are still here for a reason,* he said, looking straight ahead.

"Sa Bondye sere pou ou, lavalas pa ka pote l ale," *What God has saved for you, nobody can take away,* Rose said.

"Sa la verite," *That's the truth,* Pierre said.

When they parked in front of the house, Rose invited Pierre to come inside.

"Non, mesi. Mwen gin retounen travay. N a wè Samdi maten," *No, thank you. I have to go back to work. We'll see you Saturday morning,* Pierre said.

"Kenbe." *Hang in there.*

Rochelle stepped out and sat in the front passenger seat. Pierre would take her to Dominique's house where she would meet her daughter.

"N a wè pita," *See you later,* they said as they drove off.

Rose asked Jean Carmelo what he wanted to eat.

"Ma, I told you before we got here that I would eat minimally."

"We have to eat something!" Rose replied, scoffing.

"I only need water. What I'm most concerned about are the medications you and Dad are taking."

"I took my medication this morning. If you don't remind your father, he'll forget to take his."

"Humans can go weeks without food. We'll be fine," Jean Carmelo said nonchalantly.

"No, we're not going to starve," Rose responded.

When Jean Carmelo and Rose got inside, Lauren and Anel did their best to quietly end a disagreement they were having. Lately, they had been arguing like brother and sister. They each thought that the other should do more to help out. The increased tension on the streets was beginning to rub off on them.

Lauren had cooked up some brown rice and boiled plantains. She sat down at the table with Anel, Emmanuel, Jean Carmelo, Rose, and Jules. As they ate, Jean Carmelo was amazed by how fortunate they were. Days ago, they had been separated in one of the hardest hit areas. Now, they were reunited at the same table. Although time would tell what damage was done psychologically, no one suffered a scratch physically.

After dinner, they moved their chairs to just outside the patio and sat in the front yard. They were influenced by the radio announcer repeatedly warning against staying indoors for extended periods. The impromptu tent cities were especially vulnerable. As the sky became darker, more people joined the groups to provide strength. Throughout the night, the prayers, songs, and dancing would keep intruders and trespassers at bay.

An aftershock rumbled through the city, knocking down the small framed paintings on the living room wall. Jean Carmelo began noting the times of each tremor on his cell phone. A welcomed sensation in his lower abdomen let him know it was finally time to hit the bathroom. If he had gone another day without a bowel movement, he would have worried that he had a serious problem. The singing from the groups outside stopped as they all braced themselves, but a few seconds later, the rhythmic handclaps, tambourines, drums, congas, and shakers were louder and more intense. That went on until everyone became tired and retreated to their beds.

Jean Carmelo wanted to get as much sleep as he could before the sun rose and kept him from staying in bed. He lay down on his back with his eyes open, staring at the ceiling, on guard for the next big shock. Every time he put his head down, he heard the ground moving. It was as if giant gears were turning, shifting, searching for a position to lock in.

His parents had insisted on sleeping in the bedroom in the middle of the house. Rose still had a few quick steps left in her, but Jules remained in a daze. Jean Carmelo knew there was no way Jules could get out of the house fast enough if the aftershocks brought down the roof.

Jean Carmelo and Anel stood outside, watching from behind the wall. Men carried their deceased loved ones in thin, plywood caskets. They were searching for morgues with vacancy. At the cemeteries, bodies were being removed from above-ground tombs. Some tombs were replaced with the newly dead while others were stacked with more bodies. When men could no longer muster the strength to continue, they left the caskets on the sides of the roads. Pedestrians walked by them with their noses and mouths shielded with handkerchiefs, occasionally looking down and shaking their heads in horror.

For a couple of days, a wooden coffin had been left in front of Jean Carmelo's grandmother's house. A white rear-loader garbage truck labeled "Mairie de Carrefour" stopped where the coffin was. The driver and his two-man crew got out and walked over to the coffin while putting on white work gloves and masks. A small group of bystanders spotted them picking up the casket and began a spirited protest. They felt throwing out a body was an inhumane method of disposing of the person inside.

The men told the group they had been hired by the town to perform a job, and they had no choice but to do what they came to do. The driver answered a call on his cell phone and indicated to the other men that they were on a schedule. Somehow, they convinced two of the bystanders to help them. The five men lifted and carried the casket. They struggled to place it down on a metal platform at the rear of the truck.

The driver walked to the other side of the truck and manually operated the hydraulic valves to begin the compression. The faces of those on both sides of the street turned ugly as the metal crushed the wood. Splinters of wood sprayed out of the rear of the truck.

Jean Carmelo walked inside. Rose and Lauren were taking down the curtains. Rose put one set up at the front door, and Lauren put the other on the doorway separating the dining room from the bed and bathrooms.

"Mom, there was something I forgot to tell you while we were at the funeral home," he said.

"What is it?"

"We can't have a limo pick us up tomorrow."

"The plans have already been made. The phones are no good to change things."

"There's got to be a way. It would be disrespectful for us to drive off in a limo. You know what I mean?"

"I understand. You make a good point," she said.

"Even before this whole mess happened, I wanted to tell you that I felt uncomfortable with the whole grand appearance. The important thing is that we respectfully treat Grandma. We all know she deserves the best. We also know she wasn't flashy in how she lived her life. She would have wanted us to keep it simple."

Burial Grounds

Jean Carmelo woke up a few minutes before 6 a.m. Anel got up soon after and came out front where Jean Carmelo stood. They were both absorbed by the early street action. Reality television couldn't even come close. Word of mouth was the most reliable source of information.

As much as Jean Carmelo was intrigued by the events engulfing all of his senses, he was ready to carry on with whatever the day had in store and focus on rebuilding. His cell phone battery was low. Traveling anywhere with limited communication made him uneasy.

He turned to Anel. "Konbyen yo van-n gazolin?" *How much is gasoline?*

"Gazolin se swasanndis-senk dola Ayisyen pou yon galon," – *Gas is seventy-five Haitian dollars for one gallon,* Anel said.

"Sa a yon pri apik pou yon bagay ki te sèlman yon kèk dolar jou de sa." *That's a steep price for something that was only a few bucks days ago.* "Si nou gen gazolin, eske nou kab chaje telefòn sa-a? *If we had gas, could we charge this telephone?* He held up his cell phone.

Anel grabbed the phone and looked it over, searching for its input jack. "Ou pa gen anyen ankò pou chaje?" *Do you have anything to plug?*

"Wi, li andann." *Yes, it's inside.*

"Byen. Nou bezwen gazolin," *Fine. We need gasoline,* Anel said.

"Lè li leve m ap wè si manman mwen gen lajan," *When she wakes up, I'll see if my mother has money,* Jean Carmelo said.

"Se byen," Anel replied.

* * * *

Gradually, Rose, Jules, Emmanuel, and Lauren got up and took turns to brush their teeth and clean up in the bathroom. A makeshift buffet of bread, butter, cereal, crackers, and tea was laid out on the dining room table.

After breakfast, they all dressed and got ready. Anel, in a tan suit, was the first one dressed. Jean Carmelo was sitting outside, putting on his shoes. Anel asked him for help to properly adjust the knot on his tie. Although Jean Carmelo rarely wore a tie anymore, his muscle memory from Catholic high school was still present. Rose wore a black blouse and skirt, a black hat wrapped with a black bow, and low-cut black shoes. Rochelle wore the white dress she had retrieved from what was left of her house, white shoes, and a black dress hat. Jules had decided not to attend the funeral. He didn't feel comfortable with his limited mobility and the crowds of people.

Pierre arrived in the gold Land Cruiser. Jean Carmelo stepped out onto the patio and breathed a sigh of relief. The word about not driving the limo had gotten to him from Dominique.

Jean Carmelo poked his head inside and said, "Ma, Pierre is waiting for us."

"Okay, we're coming," Rose answered.

Rochelle, Rose, and Emmanuel walked across the living room and made their way out onto the patio. Anel was already opening the front gate. After helping Rose, Rochelle, Anel, and Emmanuel into the back seat, Jean Carmelo sat up front. They left, as planned, at seven sharp. The ride to the parlor was relatively trouble free. Few vehicles were on the road that early in the morning. Pedestrian traffic was light. Teen-aged boys curled up in the fetal position, slept on the front steps of closed businesses. Stray dogs and skinny cats roamed aimlessly.

Pierre pulled up in front of the funeral parlor and parked on a concrete hill near the entrance of the building. He and Jean Carmelo got out first and helped the ladies and Emmanuel from the back out the vehicle.

They walked into the viewing room where a few family and friends were already seated. Before them was a white coffin with gold handles and trim. Lying on top of the bottom half was a large bouquet of white, purple, and pink flowers. The top half was open. Inside, resting on soft white cotton and linen, was Jean Carmelo's grandmother.

He gathered himself for a minute, taking a calm breath of the stale air. He stepped aside, allowing everyone to pass him. He slowly followed them to view her body. When he looked into her face, every other object in the room became an insignificant blur. The embalming preservatives couldn't restore her natural appearance. He experienced an energy coming from somewhere, and they had a light, cordial conversation. Without moving his lips, he told her how much she was missed. She thanked him and let him know that it was important for him to witness all that he had in the last few days.

His memories of her began to pour out without spilling. There was the time she threw a walking cane to the floor in defiance. She had been ninety-two years young, and she had wanted to prove she could overcome discomfort in her back and legs. On other occasions, she had refused to use new cooking pots Rose sent in favor of hole-ridden aluminum pots that she had used effortlessly for decades. He remembered her soft-spoken eloquence. Those were the visions that kept him in a pleasant state.

Her expression was final, without resentment, and she seemed content, as if she had done all she wanted to do. She conveyed an eagerness to conclude her appearance on earth so she could commence the rest she'd often spoken of during her last days.

Sitting beside Emmanuel, Jean Carmelo replayed whatever he could from his grandmother's life. Playing in the background was the CD Rose had requested. Rose, with her sisters on each shoulder, remained relaxed, holding a small black purse and showing little emotion. Renee, the eldest of five children, sat in a wheelchair at the end of the row and cried hysterically. The small group of family and friends reflected on the woman they'd once known and loved.

A gentleman from the parlor walked over and whispered to Rose that the time to end the viewing was approaching. Rose looked at her watch and looked around as if she'd had an idea. Making eye contact with Jean Carmelo, she gestured for him to come closer.

"What's wrong?" he asked.

"Did you bring your camera?"

"Yeah, it's right here." He pulled out his camera from his pants pocket.

"I want you to take pictures."

The mood was somber, and he found her request a bit awkward. Rose noticed his hesitation and surprised expression.

"The parlor didn't have anyone to take pictures. I need to have memories," Rose said.

That made sense. The ceremony was Rose's way of allowing those affected by her mother's journey to reflect and remember. Pushing things along smoothly was the least he could do. He moved closer to the casket and snapped shots. He turned to take pictures of all those in attendance as they got up to leave. A small line formed as most of them approached the casket one last time to pay their respects.

The parlor workers soon came to close the casket, signaling the end of the ceremony. As everyone made their way toward the exit doors, the energy of the group transformed. In the hour they had been inside, the vehicle and foot traffic in the city had grown exponentially. The group crossed the busy street to the church directly on the other side. Shouting matches carried on as vendors sparred with buyers over goods and prices. Dust rose from mopeds and bicycles moving faster than the cars stuck in bumper-to-bumper gridlock.

They arrived at a large, shady courtyard that sloped down, leading to the large two-story yellow church. Hanging from the trees and surrounding the building were multi-colored, triangle-shaped flag banners. They saw hundreds of people gathered for a ceremony already in progress. A podium had been set up in front of the church. Two black hearses lined up facing the street. A priest spoke at the podium, facing several rows of black metal folding chairs.

Jean Carmelo and his family and friends stood back, waiting their turn, along with another small family there to mourn a deceased member. Their loved ones would be celebrated simultaneously. Many in attendance held napkins or handkerchiefs to their noses due to the stench of the bodies. Large flies buzzed around, looking to land on people. The smell and intensity of the flies would only worsen as the day got hotter.

The Bible on a stand, gold cup, and two blue candles rested on a table with a white cloth. The table's legs were raised up on broken pieces of cinder block. The priest, dressed in purple over a long-sleeved white garment, stood behind a wooden podium. Behind him were, a pair of speakers and a small PA system.

A short time later, the pallbearers lifted the caskets and carefully placed them into the hearses. The crowd began to disperse. The priest signaled for the two waiting families to come down and take their seats. Two hearses outside made their way in once the two others had cleared the way.

Jean Carmelo sat in the first row with Rose and Emmanuel. The priest, understandably anxious to begin, read a few prepared passages from the Bible. The flies were relentless pests that had to somehow be accounted for. Whether they were humming in people's ears, parking on their faces and clothes, or crawling on hands and legs, they required constant attention.

A young man and woman stood a short distance behind the priest. The woman held a small song book that they quickly reviewed. The man pressed a button on the stereo system, and the two of them stepped up to the microphone to sing some short hymns. After the songs were finished, the priest walked over to the table covered with white cloth. He stood next to the microphone behind the table and faced the crowd. An altar boy in all white came over to help hand the priest bottles of wine, water, and whatever else he needed.

Next, they were off to the burial plots. Jean Carmelo, Rose, Rochelle, Emmanuel, and Anel got in the jeep with Pierre. Dominique and the rest of the family got in another vehicle. Samuel, who also worked with the funeral parlor, said he knew where to go. The three cars formed a caravan and followed the hearse. They drove a little more than a mile before they turned off of the main road and onto a long, narrow, rugged dirt path that led to the cemetery.

The closer they got to the site where the burial would occur, the more random concrete slabs were in the road. The three cars arrived at a large lot where they could not advance any farther. Small patches of shade were provided by tall trees. A considerably more pronounced sour stench greeted them as they stepped out the vehicles. The women scrambled through their pocketbooks for napkins and pieces of cloth to shield their noses. The men dug in their pockets to retrieve handkerchiefs. Jean Carmelo removed his suit jacket and observed the cemetery.

"Jean Carmelo, we have another piece for you to cover your nose," Rose said.

"No, I'm okay, Ma."

She looked at him in awe. Jean Carmelo had become numb to the sights, sounds, and smells surrounding him. He looked off into the distance. Shaking his head, he thought of the thousands who did not have such an honorable ceremony.

A man wearing a black and white dress shirt and tie approached them. He briefly explained some confusion due to previously unheard of acts. People had been coming into the lot with hammers and shovels and removing bodies from vaults to place in their own family members. He told the group to follow him.

Four other men lifted the casket out of the hearse and transported it to the burial plot. They walked past a few aisles of large concrete columns, searching for the plot number. The four men placed the casket down in front of number 777. That would be Jean Carmelo's grandmother's final resting place.

One of the men began preparing a water and cement mix. Two men on each side grabbed the casket's gold handles, counted to three, and lifted the casket into the open space. Straining slightly, they pushed the box until it fit all the way in the vault. They closed the vault door, and the man with the cement filled the box with concrete bricks before using a hand trowel to fill the gaps with cement.

Hopefully, no one tries to open the door before the cement dries. That would be disgraceful and a cause for a dreadful, immediate action. Grandma, you have been seen for the last time by the animals on this planet. May you truly rest in peace. We love you.

BUMPER CARS

The roadways were teeming with residents. Yellow school buses and tap taps leaked puddles of oil. Old cars and trucks coughed thick, dark exhaust before breaking down, leaving traffic at a standstill. Jean Carmelo looked at the dashboard and noticed that the fuel was running low. He suggested that Pierre turn off the air conditioning for a few minutes to save energy.

Pierre switched off the ignition and powered down all of the windows, letting in a powerful blast of horrific, humid air. Each breath was an involuntary, all-out assault on their respiratory systems. Jean Carmelo unzipped his tie and squirmed to take off his shirt.

Hot-weather funerals are sure difficult to dress for. The main challenge is trying to stay comfortable while upholding a certain degree of respect for the dead.

A loud tap on the passenger side of the vehicle got everyone's attention. A short, middle-aged man pushing a wooden wheelbarrow filled with small bags and bottles of water and sugary drinks weaved around vehicles stuck in traffic. He asked if anyone was interested. Having gone without water for several hours, everyone was thirsty.

"Nou vle achte yon bagay!" *We want to buy something!* Pierre said, vigorously waving to signal the man to stop.

"Nou vle senk sak dlo glasé," *We want five bags of ice water!* Rose said, looking for money in her purse. "Se konbyen pou sa?" *How much?*

"Ven gourdes," *Twenty dollars,* the man replied.

"Konbyen?" *How much?*

"Ven gourdes, madam," the man answered, keeping an eye on his inventory while making another transaction.

"Se anpil. Ba-m you pi bon pri." *That's a lot. Give me a better price.*

"Mwen pa ka pab." *I can't do that.*

Rose handed money to Pierre, who made the exchange with the man. The man handed Pierre five pouches of water. When Rose held one, she wasn't satisfied with the way the container was sealed.

"Where this water came from?" she asked Jean Carmelo.

"It could be from the tap," Jean Carmelo guessed, giving one of the pouches a closer look.

"They could get this water from anywhere. The bag is not closed properly," Rose said.

"Return it," Jean Carmelo said.

"Mwen vle youn lòt jan," *I want another type,* Rose demanded.

"Boutèy pi chè," *Bottles are more expensive,* the man said.

"Pi chè?" *More expensive?*

"Wi," the man replied, ready to walk away.

"Ban nou senk boutèy," *Give us five bottles.* Rose said.

The man put five bottles in the outstretched hands of Mark, Rose, and Jean Carmelo. They paid the man the remaining amount. It didn't take much to twist open the caps on the bottles, but the man had vanished into the crowd.

"Kite m 'goute li." *Let me taste it*, Rose asked Jean Carmelo.

From time to time, she spoke to Jean Carmelo in Kreyol. Sometimes it was because she didn't feel the need to translate.

He handed her his open bottle.

She took a sip. "It's not bad. Taste it to see." Rose gave the bottle back.

"It doesn't taste like tap. We'll have to wait and see how we feel," Jean Carmelo said.

* * * *

Close to an hour later, they arrived at their house in Carrefour. Pierre offered to take Rochelle to Dominique's house.

"Mesi anpil!" *Thank you very much!* Rose said.

"De rien." *You're welcome.*

"À tout à l'heure," *I will see you later*, Rochelle said.

"À bientôt," *See you later*, Rose replied.

Jean Carmelo and Emmanuel walked inside and saw Jules sitting at one end of the dining room table, staring into space. Emmanuel headed to his room. Jean Carmelo knew Jules hadn't moved from his chair for hours. His plastic cup rested on the patio ledge a few feet away. Jean Carmelo came up with an idea to use the pictures in his camera to help improve his father's memory. He showed Jules some pictures he had taken of an accident he was involved in months earlier.

He asked Jules, "Do you remember when I was telling you about the deer that tried to run through my car?"

"Yeah," he said.

"Look at these." Jean Carmelo narrated each photo.

"You know, you're really, really lucky!" Jules said.

"I have been extremely fortunate." Jean Carmelo nodded.

"Where did it come from?"

"It flew out of the woods. I didn't even see it," Jean Carmelo said.

Jules shook his head. "That's terrible. You could have died."

"I know, but I made it."

"You know, you're really, really lucky!" Jules said.

"We're some of the most fortunate people in the world right now!" Jean Carmelo said.

"Yes."

"We were given another chance. We must be here for a reason."

"Yes." Jules said.

"This isn't over yet. The aftershocks keep coming, so we've gotta be ready to move." Jean Carmelo pointed at the front door for emphasis.

"Yeah."

"We should get up and walk around to stay loose and keep our bodies from getting stiff," Jean Carmelo said.

"Yeah."

Jean Carmelo was becoming frustrated. He couldn't connect with the inexpressive mask Jules wore. His look came off as controlled neutrality. Jean Carmelo was disheartened, knowing that if Jules kept settling for the path of least resistance, anyone attempting to help him would be put in danger.

"We've got to be ready for anything at any time!" Jean Carmelo said.

The walls began violently trembling. Every glass and ceramic object in the house sang its familiar rattling chorus. Jules, experiencing an untimely lapse of memory, remained seated, innocently staring into his son's eyes.

"Get up. Let's move!" Jean Carmelo commanded. Grabbing Jules's upper arms, he lifted him onto his feet.

Jules snatched his cane and took short steps forward, sliding his right foot across the floor. He moved more quickly than he had in years. As they bustled toward the front door, Jules stopped in his tracks. His shorts had begun falling down. He had been sitting at the table with his belt unbuckled. He did that to shave time in the bathroom due to a weakening bladder. Jean Carmelo pulled up his father's shorts and gently pushed him through the living room and patio. Holding Jules with one arm, Jean Carmelo kept his free hand over his head, keeping an eye on the ceiling. He guided Jules until they made it outside. Anel, Emmanuel, Rose, and Lauren were already outside. After several seconds, the trembling stopped.

The episode was the most serious shaking since Tuesday. A collective sigh of relief was mixed with prayers, chants, and nervous cries. It dawned on Jean Carmelo that Jules and his short-term memory were incommunicado. He saw firsthand what had most likely occurred with his father during the initial tremor. He had been paralyzed by fear of falling, fear of failure, and fear of fatal consequence. His instincts were clouded, no longer aiding in his survival.

"We've gotta stay outside tonight!" Jean Carmelo said as they stood under a navy blue sky peppered with bright stars.

After the hysteria began to subside, Jean Carmelo, Anel, and Emmanuel brought chairs from the patio and placed them in front of the garage. For hours, they all sat quietly, listening to the radio, reflecting on what had just happened, and guessing at what the future had in store. One by one, Jules, Lauren, and Rose went to their bedrooms for the night.

Jean Carmelo couldn't believe what he was witnessing. He turned to Rose. "Ma, you're actually gonna sleep inside?"

"Ah, Jean Carmelo, we'll be okay. I'm tired, and I have to sleep."

"I don't understand you."

"Nothing will happen. Where are you going to sleep?" she asked.

"I'm going to move my bed to the patio."

"Oh no, you can't sleep outside. It's not safe."

"You think you're safe all the way in that back room? What are you going to do when the building starts shaking again?" he asked.

"Don't worry. I will move."

"Oh yeah? What about Dad? You're gonna move with him? I don't think so."

"Don't sleep outside." She retreated to the bedroom.

They were content with their abilities—or lack thereof—to make it out if another tremble occurred during the night. By midnight, Jean Carmelo and Emmanuel were the last two sitting on the patio. Jean Carmelo stared into the sky, mentally recapping the day's events. Emmanuel sat in his chair, leaning against the patio wall with one hand curled around the iron mesh. He was exhausted and fading in and out of sleep.

Jean Carmelo turned to him and said, "Ou sanblé-w fatigé." *You seem tired.*

Emmanuel was clearly trying to be the last one to go to bed. He didn't talk much, but the frown lines of frustration were growing on his face. He must have either wanted to follow the protocol of being a good host or he wanted to make certain that all of the doors were locked. Jean Carmelo figured that it was the latter. Once Jean Carmelo had a goal in mind, he isolated solutions and dismissed possible failure. He was just as tired as Emmanuel was, but he was willing to stay up all night if he had to.

Rodeo Ride

Jean Carmelo woke early the next morning. The concerns churning in his mind allowed him no more than a few hours of light sleep. Surrounded by darkness, he remained motionless in bed with his eyes closed, enjoying the silence. When he sensed sunlight entering the room, he opened his eyes and looked though the cut-out window on the opposite wall.

He closed his eyes again and continued to rest, listening to birds searching for food on the ground, dogs shaking themselves clean, and the first people walking outside. If it was meant to be, he would make it to the airport today. Jean Carmelo heard Anel talking to someone at the front gate. It was most likely the vendor who normally set up right on the other side of the wall. They were exchanging the latest news. There was still no daily newspaper. Cell phone reception was spotty but becoming more available.

Standing outside, Jean Carmelo remembered that he needed gasoline to charge his cell phone. He got out of bed and cleaned up in the bathroom. A short while later, he walked outside. Anel was pointing to the clouds and told him that big planes had been flying around.

While standing outside, they looked up and saw a large object resembling a metal albatross gliding through the sky. Anel said it was a United States military plane heading toward the airport.

"Nasyonzini?" *United Nations?* Jean Carmelo asked.

"Wi," *Yes,* Anel replied.

Jean Carmelo felt change about to come. This trip was one thing after another big thing, but now that an international presence was near, it brought a mixture of hope and anxiety. He went inside to try to gather his thoughts.

When he sat on the bed to put on his socks, Rose walked over to him.

"Good morning, Ma," Jean Carmelo said.

"Good morning, son. You look tired. You didn't sleep?" she asked.

"No, not much."

"Why not?"

"You know, Ma. All of this stuff going on," Jean Carmelo said.

"Yes, I know. Your father slept very well."

"How do you know?"

"He snored all night. He's still sleeping. I didn't sleep much, just like you." She forced a smile.

"Ma, in order to charge the phones, we need gasoline."

"Why you telling me for? Go buy your gas," Rose said, half jokingly.

"Anel said he can get some this morning," Jean Carmelo said.

"How much is it?"

"A hundred dollars a galon."

"Oh! A hundred dollars! It's that expensive? These people are crooks!" Rose said.

"People have cars. They need gas to move."

"Are you sure that one gallon will be enough to charge all the phones? My phone needs to get charged too," Rose said.

"Yes, Ma. Anel is outside right now. We can double-check with him."

"Anel!" Rose called.

"Wi!" Anel responded, promptly coming into the living room.

"Bonjou!" *Good morning!* Rose said.

"Bonjou!" he replied.

"Mwen tande gazolin se yon santèn dola . Se vré?" *I heard gas is a hundred dollars. This is true?*

"Wi. Yon yon santèn dola ayisyen," *Yes. One hundred Haitian dollars,* Anel replied.

"Si mwen ba ou yon santèn dola l ap gen ase?" *If I give you a hundred dollars, will it be enough?*

"Wi, l ap gen ase," *Yes, there will be enough,* Anel replied.

"Ou ka achte souple?" *Can you buy some please?*

"Wi, M ap achte I." *Yes, I will buy some.*

Rose reached into her purse and pulled out the necessary amount. She handed it to Anel.

"Merci," he replied, taking the money and walking out the door to retrieve an empty plastic container.

Jean Carmelo turned the radio on at a low volume, got his bags, and began packing his things. The news coming through the radio caught his attention. The speaker said something about the possibility that flights leaving the country would resume that day. Jean Carmelo wondered whether or not his plane ticket would be honored if he left at another time. Leaving was a monumental decision. Once he left, there was no turning back.

Anel returned with a full container of gasoline. He went to the side of the house where the generator was located, and Emmanuel helped him find the extension cords to set it up. Jean Carmelo got his cell phone and Rose's. Anel enjoyed applying his craftiness to electronics, so he figured out the right combination of wires and plugs to use while Emmanuel poured the gas into the generator. When Anel plugged in the cell phones, Jean Carmelo pulled on the zip cord to start the motor. On the third try, the motor gave a loud mumble and started. Anel motioned to Jean Carmelo that it would be a slow process, but eventually all of the phones would be charged. Jean Carmelo went inside and sat on the couch. With his hands clasped behind his head, he meditated for a moment.

Rose walked in. "I've been trying to call Jacques, but the line is always busy."

"Do you really have to stay until next week?" Jean Carmelo asked.

"Oh yes. I have to see if I can get the doctor for Emmanuel's eye surgery. Nobody knows if the doctor is dead or alive," Rose replied with defiant confidence.

"I know you care about your brother, but let's say that you can't find this doctor. "

"I don't know when I'm going to come back here. I have to take care of all of my business now."

"Seven more days here is a long time," he said.

"I have to make sure that everything is taken care of."

"I'm gonna go crazy not knowing how you are. The communication is garbage."

"I'll be okay. I don't know about your father," his mother said.

"I know. Who's going to help him?"

"He's going to have to help himself. He insisted on coming."

"I don't trust him around crowds," Jean Carmelo said.

"Don't worry about us. You don't have time to waste. We still don't know who's going to take you to the airport."

"Didn't you tell me that the neighbor's nephew has a motorcycle?"

"YesHe went out. The mother said she would let me know when he came back. Let me go over and see if he's there. I'll ask Emmanuel if he knows anyone. Make sure your bags are packed," Rose said.

"Okay. Is there a telephone book here? I'll see if I can call American Airlines."

"YesLook on top of the refrigerator."

"I see it."

"Okay, I'll be back," she said before she walked out the door.

Jean Carmelo opened up the weather-beaten telephone book from 2008. Scanning its pages, he engaged an intimidating French lexicon he had not attempted to make sense of since his second year in college. He flipped through, looking for pictures. He came across a few pictures of airplanes under the letter "C" for "compagnie aérienne." He stepped out to use his cell phone and started calling each of the dozen 800-numbers listed underneath American Airlines. With each number, he was greeted by an unusually low voice speaking French. Then he remembered that he kept the American Airlines 800-number in his cell phone. Jules and Rose traveled frequently, so he kept it for emergencies. He dialed the number but was disconnected. It was time for plan B.

Waiting for Rose to come back, Jean Carmelo brought his two bags and the last of his unpacked items out to the patio. He imagined himself on the back of a motorcycle with his bags hanging over his shoulders. How would he pull that off in those streets? The most important pieces of his life weren't the material things he was packing. He would soon be leaving his family.

As soon as he was done packing, he took a metal chair outside and placed it in front of the garage. He took off his shirt and sat down to catch some rays, soaking up every last piece of the roots of his existence. The sun's warmth was as inviting as ever. His experience in Haiti had been blissful in many ways, despite the conditions. He knew he may not return anytime soon. He may never see that place again.

Emmanuel and Anel also felt it. It was written in their stoic postures and expressions. The three of them posted themselves in the front yard in a triangle formation. Jean Carmelo sat in front of the garage, Emmanuel was a few feet away by a tree, and Anel was at the front gate, looking out toward the street. Each of them was silent, occupied with the thoughts swirling through their minds.

Rose came back. "I just spoke to her. She said her nephew would be back in one hour, and he will be able to take you. Get ready!"

"Thanks, Ma," Jean Carmelo replied, realizing how crazy the idea was.

Mario, a stony-voiced, middle-aged man who worked with Emmanuel, came through the front gate. He said he knew a driver who could make the trip to the airport in less than thirty minutes.

"Fè m konnen lè w prale," *Let me know when you are leaving,* Mario said.

"Le pli vit ke posib," *As soon as possible,* Jean Carmelo replied, looking at his watch.

"Konbyen li koute?" *How much does it cost?* Rose asked.

"Ban-m' gade. M ap chaché konnen. M ap rele li koulnyé-a." *Let me see. I will find out. I'll call him now.* He pulled out his cell phone from his pants pocket.

Jean Carmelo and Rose looked at each other, both knowing that whoever was on the other line would be able to make the trip.

"Nou pare?" *Are you ready?* Mario asked.

"Wi," Jean Carmelo replied.

"Li koute de san dola Ameriken," *It will cost two hundred American dollars,* Mario said.

"Mezanmi! Li chè!" *Wow! That's expensive!* Rose responded.

"Do you have enough money to last for another week? I've got a hundred dollars in my pocket if you've got another hundred," Jean Carmelo said to Rose.

"Ou ka ban-m you pi bon pri souple?" *Can you please give me a better price?* Rose asked Mario. "I paid a hundred dollars for Jacques to bring us here from the airport," Rose said to Jean Carmelo.

"No, madam, gazolin yon santèn dola Ayisyen pou yon gallon," *No, ma'am, gasoline is a hundred Haitian dollars for a gallon,* Mario replied.

"Okay, di li met vin," *Okay, tell him he can come over,* Rose said.

"Li di ou met vini," *She said you can come now,* Mario said into his phone.

"I want to go to the airport with you," Rose said.

"Nan ki tan li ka vin isit la?" *At what time can he come here?* Jean Carmelo asked.

"L ap rive la nan kenz minit," *He'll be here in fifteen minutes,* Mario said.

"Mesi anpil!" *Thank you very much!* Jean Carmelo said.

Everything had doubled in price over the past few days. Making such a large commitment felt strange to Jean Carmelo. *Why am I so eager to leave? Why is mom so insistent on staying?*

Fifteen minutes later, a burgundy Nissan Pathfinder pulled up out front of the house.

"Ou vini alé. Ki gen ou rele?" *You came at perfect time. What is your name?* Rose said, sounding surprised.

"M'rele Patrick." *My name is Patrick.* He shook their hands.

"M'rele Rose. Sa se Jean Carmelo," *My name is Rose. This is Jean Carmelo,* Rose said.

"Nou pare?" *Are you ready?* Patrick asked.

The spiritual signals that normally told Jean Carmelo what to do next were distorted, blurred by his inability to focus long enough to let them communicate with him. Time was running out. The ticket he was holding said the plane was scheduled to depart at 11:45 am. They had exactly 45 minutes. There was a part of him that wanted to leave that hot wasteland. Another part of him was bothered by the lack of emotion from Jules. Jules sat glued to the chair, appearing as if he had almost given up on keeping up with the changes around him.

Jean Carmelo walked over to him and gave him a tight hug. "I'll miss you, Dad. I'm gonna see if I can get on one of these planes."

"Okay. Did you get everything?" Jules asked.

"Yes, I got everything. I love you."

"Okay. Don't keep them waiting," Jules said.

Jean Carmelo walked out front and put his bags into the back of Patrick's jeep. He hugged Emmanuel and Anel. Rose wanted to sit in the back between two of Patrick's friends. Patrick got behind the wheel, and Jean Carmelo took shotgun. They peeled off.

There was no turning back. Jean Carmelo had given his decision a good deal of thought, and all of the different scenarios he played out in his mind came to the same conclusion: He should leave. He couldn't force his parents to go if they weren't ready.

Patrick tore through the streets. He made good use of his horn in typical Port-au-Prince fashion as he dodged animals, vendors, and mechanics working on vehicles parked on the street.

Rose tapped Jean Carmelo's left shoulder. He turned around and looked at her.

"Is your seat belt on?" she asked nervously, clutching the front seat.

"Yes, Ma, my seatbelt is on," Jean Carmelo replied.

He understood her concern. He was attempting to keep his cool too. Traffic heading out of Port-au-Prince was backed up for miles. Patrick took matters into his own hands, honking and driving on the wrong side of concrete medians dividing the road. Oncoming traffic was much lighter, allowing them to pass more than a hundred cars. Thick clouds of gray and black smoke filled the sky. The road was blocked with dozens of people arguing over something.

Patrick put down his window and asked a tall young man, "Qu'est ce que c'est?" *What is this about?*

"Genyen moun la-yo k ap boule kò," *There are people over there burning bodies,* the young man replied.

Dead bodies were lined up in the middle of the road. Those not covered with white sheets were being burned in the street. Traffic was jammed for long stretches, but nothing seemed to slow down their driver. When one route was blocked off, Patrick knew of a plan B or plan C. Without hesitation, he made sharp three-point turns before skidding in the opposite direction. Side streets were no longer an option. Narrow alleyways between the crumbling walls were congested with trauma.

On the main roads, entire blocks of hotels, restaurants, bars, and houses were destroyed. They cooked down the road at speeds over 100 mph. Jean Carmelo couldn't believe they were moving so fast. If they were in anything other than an SUV, the roads would have devoured their vehicle. All four tires left the ground as they flew over small hills and deep holes. Not much of anything was said during the ride. They continued to bounce up and down as Patrick swayed left and right around obstacles.

Rose sat in the back, squeezing her eyes shut and clenching her teeth. As much as she tried to keep her composure, she couldn't help clutching the seat in front of her or the two men beside her. Jean Carmelo got the impression that not only was Patrick a stunt man, but his partners had been along for the ride a hundred times before. The two men barely raised an eyebrow when the jeep came within inches of taking out a pedestrian.

Jean Carmelo's jaw hung open when he saw the National Palace. Word of mouth had described the area as badly damaged, but seeing it up close was shocking. The palace was completely destroyed. There was a large yard between the building and the iron gates that separated it from the streets. The interior appeared dark and dusty. Maybe that explained the lack of presence from the elected officials. The fallen symbol cemented the idea that the country would never be the same again.

The area surrounding the National Palace was one of the few with working traffic signals. But their driver wasn't the follow-the-rules type. While other drivers waited on lights to turn green, he sped by, weaving in and out of traffic. *What a rush!* On his most fearless day, Jean Carmelo could only imagine pulling off something like that.

They came upon another road block that again forced them to take an alternate route. Patrick made a U-turn. Jean Carmelo looked at his watch. It was now 11:35 am. He might not make it. On an open stretch of rocky road, pushing speeds of over 90 mph, Patrick honked every fifty yards or so to warn people up the road. Bystanders froze before crossing.

On the way through Cite Soleil, they passed outdoor markets selling fruit and vegetables. Light steam and grey smoke wafted from makeshift grills. Stagnant grey puddles of waste water were sprinkled throughout the streets. It was Jean Carmelo's first time in that part of town. Not long before his grandmother's birthday, he had seen a special on *60 Minutes* about that area. The news crew had gone there with Wyclef Jean, a famous Haitian performer. They focused on his philanthropic efforts and interest in providing jobs.

Seeing it in person, Jean Carmelo wasn't surprised that many had labeled Cite Soleil the "most dangerous city in the world." The people had nothing to do all day and nothing to lose. Jean Carmelo shook his head, marveling at how, a few months ago, he had been watching that neighborhood on a television screen. The smoking slums were as grim as what the television had shown.

They were entering the parking lot of the Toussaint L'Ouverture International Airport. The building was surrounded by police. A few minutes later, Patrick pulled up to the check-in booth where a uniformed Haitian police officer stood.

He motioned for Patrick to come closer. "Konbyen moun kap vole jodi a?" *How many people are flying today?*

"Yon sèl," *One only,* Patrick said.

"Ki moun?" *Who?* the man asked, looking inside the vehicle.

"Limenm sèlman," *Only him,* Patrick, Rose, and the two men responded.

"Eske li pale kreyol?" *Does he speak Kreyol?* the officer asked.

"Li konprann," *He understands,* Rose said.

"Paspò ak tike ou souple," *Your passport and ticket please,* the man said, extending his hand toward Jean Carmelo.

Jean Carmelo handed him his passport. The officer examined the booklet and stepped closer to give Jean Carmelo a look. For a moment, he seemed to believe the person in the picture and the person in front of him weren't the same. Then he handed the passport back to Jean Carmelo. The officer pointed toward the drop-off point. He told Patrick that whoever was not traveling would not be allowed to stay for more than a few minutes. He emphasized that any attempt to park would subject them to being arrested and/or their vehicle towed.

They drove farther until a fence prevented them from going closer to the building. Patrick and his friends stayed in the vehicle to keep from violating any of the strictly enforced laws.

Jean Carmelo got out and retrieved his two bags from the back. He walked over to the driver's side. "Mesi anpil!" *Thank you very much!* Jean Carmelo gave Patrick a firm handshake.

"Veye zo ou," *Be careful,* Patrick replied.

Mario and Rose stepped out of the jeep to accompany Jean Carmelo to the line.

"Pa bliye nou pa genyen unpil tan," *Don't forget we don't have a lot of time,* Patrick said, looking in his rearview mirror at the officer.

Scores of people stood outside the main building. The line extended about a quarter of a mile away from the building. Jean Carmelo looked at the time on his cell phone. He had less than twenty minutes before his flight was scheduled to leave. He told Mario and Rose to hold his spot in line, and he jogged to the front of the line. Two United States soldiers, dressed in camouflage uniforms with rifles slung over their shoulders, stood with authoritative swagger.

Jean Carmelo approached them. "Hi. I've got a flight on American Airlines scheduled to leave in fifteen minutes. I need to get through this line." Jean Carmelo held out his ticket.

"For all flights, you'll have to wait in that line," one soldier said, pointing at the long line Jean Carmelo had just come from.

"I won't make the flight on time!" Jean Carmelo said.

"That's the only line coming in this building," he calmly replied.

Disappointed, Jean Carmelo headed back to Rose and Mario. He had little choice but to stay in line. Since his brief time talking to the soldiers, twenty more people had joined the line. Jean Carmelo thanked Mario for finding him a ride.

Patrick honked from the parking lot with a look that suggested their time was up.

"Nou prale koulnyé-a," *We are leaving now,* Rose said.

"Okay, Ma, I know you've gotta go."

Rose looked at him while holding back tears as best she could. "I'm going to miss you. Stay strong and be careful. I gave you the phone numbers, yes?"

"Yes, I have them," Jean Carmelo replied.

"I don't know when we will speak again. Pray for us," she said.

"You'll always stay right here." He pointed at his heart.

"Make sure you keep an eye on your bags! Do you have all your papers?"

"Yes, they're with me."

"Keep them safe. I love you dearly," she said.

"I love you too, Ma."

They hugged tightly, but in a second, they released each other. So many thoughts raced through Jean Carmelo's brain as Rose and Mario walked off. *When will I see her again? How will Dad react—or will he react—during another aftershock?* Jean Carmelo followed them with his eyes until they got back to the vehicle. Rose turned around and waved good-bye, just like he knew she would. He waved back. She got inside, and the jeep pulled off.

It didn't take long for Jean Carmelo's survival skills to be tested. A man who got in line behind him minutes earlier somehow managed to weasel in front of Jean Carmelo. Without hesitation, Jean Carmelo grabbed his bags and regained his spot.

"Ki sa wop fè? Mwen te la anvan!" *What are you doing? I was here before!* the man shouted.

"Sa pa vre. Ou té wè mwen kanpé la devan ou!" *That's not true. You saw me standing in front of you!* Jean Carmelo replied, raising his voice to an even volume.

Jean Carmelo was not about to tolerate being cheated. He stood firm in a loose fighting stance. He had already made the decision that the man would not pull off the ol' switcheroo. A nearby acquaintance of the man took on the role of mediator, stepping in before the situation escalated.

"Kité sa," *Relax! Let it go,* the mediator said, placing his palm on the man's chest.

"Mwen te genyen dé moun kanpé la pou mwen!" *I had two people standing here for me!* Jean Carmelo explained.

The mediator listened to the man claim that Jean Carmelo had come ten minutes after he did and rudely got in front of him. The mediator turned to Jean Carmelo. "Nou pa genyen problem la." *We don't have any problem here.*

"Gade pou wè," *Wait and see,* the man mumbled.

"Mwen vle fé zanmi avèk tout moun," *I want to be friends with everyone,* the mediator said calmly.

"Dakò." *Agreed.* Jean Carmelo nodded to keep from adding unnecessary fuel to the fire. He felt the tension still bubbling but gradually decreasing. Jean Carmelo let his reduced aggression speak more effectively than his minimal Kreyol. From the look of things, they would be in line for a while, so he would not give off any more negative energy.

The line into the building moved a few inches every fifteen minutes. The sun intensified as noon approached. At the front of the line was a Haitian woman holding a clipboard. She took the place of the soldiers who were there earlier. People handed her their passports to be checked. She announced in Kreyol and English that only citizens from the United States or guardians of children from the U.S. would be permitted to leave the country. Jean Carmelo expected that news to discourage those who did not fit that description, but he was wrong. One of the reasons the line was moving so slowly was because an overwhelming number of people were pleading for authorities to make exceptions to the rule. U.S. soldiers worked in shifts and occasionally removed non-compliant individuals from the line.

A foreign television crew circulated through the crowd, looking for someone to talk to. One man in his early forties held a large camera on his shoulder. Another held a microphone and determined who and where they would shoot. He made eye contact with Jean Carmelo and came over, signaling for his cameraman to follow.

"Are you a native? Do you speak Kreyol?" the reporter asked.

"A little bit. I can understand more than I speak," Jean Carmelo replied.

The reporter seemed disappointed to hear Jean Carmelo's New York accent. He thanked Jean Carmelo for his time and continued his search.

Jean Carmelo noticed that the line had only moved a handful of yards in almost an hour. Standing a short distance away was another U.S. soldier. Not many people could speak to him, because he didn't seem familiar with Kreyol. That contributed to the intimidating appearance he and his fellow soldiers gave off.

When the line moved again, Jean Carmelo approached him. "Hello."

"Hi," the soldier replied.

"Do you know anything about which flights are leaving today?" Jean Carmelo asked.

"No, I haven't been told much about the departing flights."

"I had a flight scheduled for today, but I don't know what's going on."

"The personnel inside can probably tell you."

"Is this your first time here?" Jean Carmelo asked.

"Yes, it is. I served in Iraq, a tour in Afghanistan, came back to the States, and now I'm here. I've never witnessed death like this. It's awful, man! You're lucky to be alive."

"I know. I'd never seen a dead body before I came here," Jean Carmelo said.

A voice over the soldier's walkie-talkie summoned him to assist with an unknown emergency inside the building.

"I've gotta head inside. Best of luck to you, man!" the soldier said.

"All right. Take care."

Another hour had ticked by when Jean Carmelo looked at his watch. The line kept moving at a snail's pace. Each time he looked back, the line had grown exponentially. The front of the line was finally in clear view. A middle-aged woman yelled before falling on her hand and hip. She complained to anyone who would listen about her chest pains. Her husband and a U.S. soldier quickly came over, pulling her off to the side for medical treatment. Moments before she fell down, the woman holding a clipboard had told her she would not be able to fly out.

"Ou kwè sa la p di-a?" *You believe what she's saying?* one man asked.

"L ap bay manti!" *She's telling a lie!* another man said.

More people in line were skeptical about the woman's condition. They began voicing their opinions to the individuals in charge.

"Pa pèdi tan avèk moun sa!" *Don't waste time with these people!* A middle-aged woman yelled.

People in line thought that others were taking advantage of the situation by making up stories in attempts to bend the rules. They thought that every time the authorities listened to someone's sad story, the other people waiting paid the price. A short while later, two military personnel helped the woman off of the floor and into a wheelchair. Crying, she was wheeled inside the building. Her husband followed.

The closer Jean Carmelo got to the building, the more he noticed the maneuvers people were using to get through. Some were using their cell phones to get people to bring them children while others cried and pleaded their cases.

At the front of the line, a Haitian woman asked Jean Carmelo for his passport. She was assisted by a Haitian man who told Jean Carmelo to walk to the other side of the airport to enter the building. With his passport in hand, he walked along the tall, mirrored windows. He passed another soldier in the parking lot. Wearing dark sunglasses, the soldier directed him to another line a hundred yards away. *Another line? What's going on?*

Jean Carmelo approached the line that was not nearly as long as the other one. It was moving a little faster and actually entering the building. The plane he'd been hoping to board would have left minutes ago. The line moved down a dark, narrow hallway. Streaks of sunlight came through the windows in the rear of the room, revealing cracks in the walls and ceilings. It was no wonder why the line moved more quickly than the one outside.

Two dozen people, mainly Caucasians, had just gotten off of a plane. They tried to pass Jean Carmelo, going in the opposite direction. As the line turned the corner, he saw two ladies in uniform sitting at a table near the doors to the tarmac. They were checking U.S. passports for a second time.

"Paspò ou souple!" *Your passport please!* one of them asked with her hand extended in Jean Carmelo's direction.

He handed her his booklet. The wind from the large aircraft outside blew into the building. When he was given back his passport, he felt a step closer to entering another stage of this journey.

On the tarmac, three lines of men, women, and children meshed into one along the edges of the building. The murmur and constant chatter made one thing clear: no one knew what was going on! Jean Carmelo was beyond thirsty. He noticed a young woman in front of him drinking a small, blue bottle of water.

"Do you mind if I ask where you got water around here?" He pointed at the bottle in her hand, not knowing if she spoke English.

"Laba a," *Over there,* she replied, pointing at a gentleman wearing a white hard hat and an orange reflective vest.

"Merci." He placed his bags down behind the women in front of him and approached the man. "Do you have any water?"

"Sure, we do." He reached into a tall blue container directly in front of him.

"Thank you," Jean Carmelo said, accepting the cold bottle.

"You're welcome, sir."

"My flight with American Airlines was scheduled to leave today. Do you know which one of these planes is headed to New York?" Jean Carmelo asked.

"I'm sorry. I don't have any information on where these planes are going."

"Okay. Thanks for the water."

"It's the least I can do," the man replied.

Jean Carmelo twisted off the cap and drank the entire bottle in two big gulps. He felt his organs marching in appreciation as the chilly sensation rushed down his throat to the bottom of his empty stomach. Soon after, those in line behind him asked for water as well.

The three lines ahead of him were filled with people trying to squeeze their way closer to the departure tents. A middle-aged woman dragged two bulky suitcases. Accompanying her were two energetic twin boys. They kicked around a soccer ball on the carousel conveyer belt.

Many large military aircraft from Brazil, Columbia, Israel, Canada, Norway, Russia, and various other countries were out on the strip. That was when it hit Jean Carmelo that the entire world had heard about the earthquake. He pulled out his camera, but when he pressed the power button, the screen read "low battery" before shutting off. The camera had completely run out of power. Standing behind him was a man in his early twenties. He wore a grey and red backpack on his chest and carried another tan bag. He looked like an American. Hanging around his neck was a small Canon digital camera.

"Hey, you speak English?" Jean Carmelo asked without hesitation.

"Yeah."

"My name is Jean Carmelo."

"I'm Marc," he replied as they shook hands.

"Were you in the earthquake?" Jean Carmelo asked.

"Not really. I came from Saint-Marc."

"I've never heard of it. Where's that?"

"It's north of here and off toward the western coast," Marc said.

"You didn't feel anything at all?" Jean Carmelo said in astonishment.

"Not a thing. Where were you?"

"My family and I were right in the middle of it. We were in Port-au-Prince!"

"Wow! Is everyone all right?" Marc asked.

"We all made it out alive. We were on the first floor of a two-story building. How crazy is that?" Jean Carmelo said.

"That's incredible! You're really lucky."

"I know."

"Is your family here?" Marc asked.

"No, my mom and pop are staying in Port-au-Prince for another week," Jean Carmelo said.

"I hope they get back safe."

"Thanks, man. I hope so too."

The powerful roar from the engines spawned a warm wind tunnel and commanded attention from everyone. Jean Carmelo noted scads of long cracks and chipped concrete on the exterior walls of the air traffic control tower. He started coming up with a plan of action in case a tremble should weaken the building further. Sprinting toward the wide open tarmac seemed like the obvious choice. As the mighty aircraft continued to hum, he wondered if anyone would even feel an aftershock until the building started coming down.

He turned to Marc. "Do you see those cracks in the building?" Jean Carmelo pointed at the cracks on the walls.

"Yeah, I did see that. Did you see up there?" Marc pointed at cracks on the airport control tower.

"Wow! I didn't even see that. Does your camera work? I didn't bring the charger for mine." Jean Carmelo held up his camera.

"Yeah, it should."

"I want to take some pictures of all of this. Can we exchange information and you can email them to me?"

"Okay, that's cool." Marc removed the camera strap from around his neck.

"Your camera looks similar to mine," Jean Carmelo said.

"Yeah, this is the button to zoom and focus. Hit this one to take the picture," Marc said, pointing at the function buttons.

"Cool, I got it." Jean Carmelo turned around to snap pictures of the airport and the scenery.

"So where are you flying to?" Marc asked.

"I'm trying to get to New York. Where are you headed?" Jean Carmelo replied.

"I live with my parents in Florida."

"I was down in Tamarac before I flew over here."

"Someone told me earlier that these planes were flying to the Dominican Republic," Marc said.

"I'm sure most of these people are trying to get somewhere in the States."

"You're right about that."

"No one has been able to tell me anything. How come none of these people know what's going on?" Jean Carmelo said.

"You must have gotten here around the same time I did, right? Marc said.

"I've been here since eleven a.m. It's almost six p.m." Jean Carmelo looked at his watch.

A couple of airport representatives started handing out stapled packets of paper to those in line. Jean Carmelo and Marc each took one.

"What's this for?" Marc asked no one in particular.

"I think one of them said it's for borrowing money from the government," Jean Carmelo replied, reading through it.

Jean Carmelo was suddenly reminded of his lack of cash. His last hundred dollars had been spent for the ride to the airport. Banks had either been destroyed or closed. The thought of traveling to an unknown destination without any money was unsettling. The paper he was holding was an emergency loan application and evacuation documentation form from the U.S. Department of State. A line on the second page asked him to declare an amount to receive and promise to repay within ninety days. After thinking about it for a few minutes, he wrote five thousand dollars. Without knowing what country or state he would land in, he figured that would cover his travel expenses.

After another hour of standing in the same spot, he began to move. One of the two tents cleared out as a small group of passengers walked out to a tan military plane. In between the two tents was a podium where a woman was checking passports again and asking people where they were looking to travel. Any kind of forward movement seemed promising. At that point, he was ready and willing to fly to any state.

When he got to the woman's podium, he leaned over and yelled as clearly as he could, "I have an American Airlines ticket that says my plane should've taken off hours ago."

"I understand, sir," she replied, giving him no indication that she could do anything.

"I filled out this paper. It says I have to borrow money for airfare and hotels? What about the ticket I brought?"

"You'll have to contact the airline and discuss that with them, sir. Where are you traveling?"

"New York," he said.

"Okay, behind me is the plane heading to the United States. When I find out where, I'll let you know, but I believe it's going to Seattle, Washington or Orlando, Florida. From there, it would be up to you to make your final travel plans," she said.

"Thank you. That was the most information I've been able to get all day." He mustered up the energy to smile.

"You're welcome," she said, returning the smile.

"Do I give this form to you?"

"No, hold on to that. You may need it when you arrive."

Jean Carmelo picked up his bags and walked over to the first of the two tents. Hundreds of passengers were either standing around or sitting on metal, foldable chairs.

When the tent filled up, the airport personnel stopped the rest of the line. Jean Carmelo tried to imagine an area that would allow him to reach a point of calm. That was not possible without his parents. He couldn't fathom peace and calm in the wake of the destruction and tragedy he'd witnessed. He wanted to think that everything would turn out all right and return to some sense of normalcy, but the raging battle between his exterior calm and internal anguish felt like acid oozing out of each and every pore.

He watched in awe as large turbines roared at a deafening volume. Their ferocious power remained tamed, stationary on the tarmac for hours upon hours. He motioned for Marc to come closer. "Hey, can you take a picture of me with the planes in the background?"

"Sure," Marc answered.

"I'm going to sit in this chair. You can take it whenever you're ready."

Marc crouched down, making sure to capture the chair Jean Carmelo was sitting in and the wings of the C-17 behind him. Jean Carmelo leaned forward, placing his index fingers in his ears to block out as much of the noise from the planes as possible.

"Good. Hold that right there," Marc said, snapping photos.

"Let me see what they look like!" Jean Carmelo replied, eager to see the pictures.

"Just press this arrow button to scroll ahead."

"These are pretty good. You've gotta send me them as soon as you can."

"Take some of me too," Marc said, posing in the same spot.

"Okay, it's on auto-focus right?"

"Yeah, just hit the silver button on the top."

Taking pictures was a good way to temporarily distract themselves. No one came to give them any information on what was going on. More hours passed as men, women, and children waited for anything. Elderly evacuees slept in their wheelchairs. Millions of dollars' worth of donated medical supplies and food stood on wooden pallets. Men and women unloaded them from the cargo planes. A group of uniformed Columbian Red Cross members huddled together to work out a plan. Fuel trucks, forklifts, military jeeps, cranes, police SUVs, and a variety of other vehicles scurried back and forth. News reporters and cameramen walked around in search of a story. Jean Carmelo stared out into the distance as the sun dipped behind the mountains.

A reporter smiled and walked over. "Hi! Do you speak English?"

"Yes," he replied.

"My name is Ron," he said, crouching down with a microphone in his hand.

"Hello, Ron," Jean Carmelo replied, a bit wary of the approaching cameraman.

"What's your name?"

"Jean Carmelo."

"We just got off that C-17 over there," Ron said. "Maybe you guys will end up going back with us."

"Who do you work for?" Jean Carmelo asked.

"We do a radio show out in Seattle. Would you mind talking on camera about what you've seen?" Ron asked.

"I'd rather not. It's not that I don't wanna talk. I just don't feel like being in front of a camera right now," Jean Carmelo said.

"No problem." He motioned to his cameraman to put down his equipment. "How long have you been here?"

"Since before eleven a.m.," Jean Carmelo said.

"What brought you to Haiti? Were you vacationing?"

"No, I was here for my grandmother's funeral."

"I'm sorry to hear that. My condolences to you and your family," Ron replied.

"Thank you."

"So are you here by yourself?" Ron asked.

"I came here with my parents."

"Are they here now?"

"No, they're still at my grandmother's house," Jean Carmelo said.

"Do they live here in Haiti?"

"They live in the States. They wanted to stay here with the rest of my family."

"Wow!"

"We went by the departure information on our plane tickets, man! I wish I could talk with them and try to urge them to come here," Jean Carmelo said.

A woman wearing an orange vest came up to Jean Carmelo. "I'm gonna need everyone to form a line behind this gentleman here." She stood in the spot where she wanted the line to begin.

"Well, it looks like you're finally about to board, man. We'll be on the same plane, so maybe we'll talk when we land in Orlando," Ron said.

"Okay, I'll see you later," Jean Carmelo said.

Those who didn't understand English sure knew what it meant to see the line start moving. Another woman wearing an orange vest counted the people in line. A little pushing and shoving occurred as parents made sure they weren't separated from their children. No one wanted to get left behind.

"Make sure to bring all of your belongings. We're getting on this plane right over there," she said, pointing at the cargo plane.

The gates opened, and they were escorted to the waiting aircraft. Jean Carmelo led the way, and the plane got bigger and bigger the closer they got. He stared in awe at the beast of an aircraft. Under the U.S. Air Force letters was a set of stairs leading to the interior. A few uniformed crew members stood along the side, directing them to the rear cargo entrance.

A crew member signaled for the line to stop. "Wait right here, sir."

"Is there a problem?" Jean Carmelo asked.

"We have to board the disabled and elderly passengers first," she said.

Crew members went to the back of the line and helped bring them to the front. Halfway between the tent and the plane, another line formed and proceeded to the plane. Dozens of reporters and cameramen from all over the world waited along the edge of the plane's entrance ramp. Military airmen in green fatigues collected bags and brought them in before allowing any passengers onboard. They boarded the most severely injured, the elderly, and the wheelchair-bound passengers.

The able-bodied stood anxiously, waiting their turn to enter. Along the walls inside of the aircraft were black and yellow seats with seatbelt harnesses. An elderly woman, her head wrapped in white bandages, screamed in agony. She held an oversized pocketbook with one hand and her heavily bandaged knee with the other as two officers lifted her wheelchair onto the plane.

Jean Carmelo stood at the tip of the ramp with his small black bag over his shoulder. Behind him were dozens of people as restless as he was. He took a few steps up and was stopped by a staff sergeant.

"Who are you here with, sir?" the sergeant asked.

"It's just me," Jean Carmelo answered.

"We've got to board those with priority right now, sir."

"I understand," Jean Carmelo responded.

It became apparent to him how many elderly and injured were there. The seats reserved for what seemed like an endless line of them filled up quickly. The airmen sat families with children on the floor in the middle of the plane. More and more people passed him. Thirty minutes earlier, he had been the first one in line. Now, he stood at the entrance, waiting for what appeared to be forever. Every time he made the slightest motion to board, he was denied.

Maybe I'm not supposed to get on this plane after all. If I don't get on this plane, I'll have no chance to contact anyone. I'll be stranded. What if they tell me I have to wait until the next flight? I'll go crazy! Who knows when the next airlift will be? This is hell on earth. I've gotta get on this plane.

His understanding and patience was being tested. Everyone onboard surely deserved to be there ahead of him. It appeared obvious that if anyone was able to make the sacrifice and stay behind, it was him. But he decided that he wasn't going to come that far only to turn around.

The sergeant waved him onboard. With quick action and a sigh of relief, Jean Carmelo walked on. The interior of the C-17 was straight out of a sci-fi movie. Brightly lit and thoroughly ventilated with cool air, the plane's high, rounded ceiling was a complex network of tubing, wires, and pipes. Gauges, handles, hooks, vents, extinguishers, and compartments were everywhere.

Jean Carmelo took the next available place on the cold metal floor. With his bag by his side, he looked around. The plane was filling up. About ten rows of people behind him, Marc helped a disabled woman communicate with an officer. Sitting next to Jean Carmelo were fellow evacuees. They were all happy to be heading in another direction.

A short, middle-aged man who pointed at his wife and son, already sitting down, was the last person allowed to board. The plane was at full capacity. A sea of photographers and journalists stood in the back, taking their last pictures and jotting notes on their writing pads. Some stayed on, and others got off for other assignments. The flight crew made great efforts to chain large pieces of heavy equipment onto the floor's metal handles.

The pilots and crew stood in the front and introduced themselves. They described how long each had been a member of the armed forces. Their jovial mood indicated that they generally enjoyed their careers. After giving a bit of information about the plane, the pilot told everyone their destination was Orlando, Florida, and the expected duration of the flight was a little under three hours.

Going through a mental list of contacts he knew in that area, Jean Carmelo thought about his former college roommate, Rodney. He had just moved to Jacksonsville with his wife and daughter. They had spoken a few weeks earlier on New Year's Day. Jean Carmelo took out his cell phone and gave him a call. He expressed his condolences and told Jean Carmelo that if he needed anything, he would be there. Jean Carmelo promised to keep him posted.

The crew told everyone seated to place the cargo straps over their laps to keep them secure during any turbulence. They announced that they were ready to take off, and the pilots went through a door to the cockpit.

Jean Carmelo looked at his watch. It was ten minutes past eight. He had been at the airport for over nine hours. The mighty turbines had been spinning for at least that long. That wasn't what he'd envisioned before he got to Haiti. He couldn't have imagined anything so berserk in his most outrageous nightmares.

For every incredible story he could tell about his experience there, someone onboard would understand. He saw the shining spirit in each and every one of them. The cabin was quiet with anticipation as the plane began to move. He was obviously not the only one about to fly without windows for the first time.

He stood and asked one of the crewmen, "Excuse me, but I've gotta use the bathroom."

"Okay, but you've got to be quick. We're minutes from taking off."

Jean Carmelo followed him toward the front of the aircraft.

"The door is right over there." He pointed.

Jean Carmelo stepped into one of two port-a-potties and shut the door. A powerful roar started in the planes massive engines. He took a couple of deep breaths and thanked nature for bringing him that far. A sudden rush of blood flooded his face, and corrosive pain simmered in his temples. He couldn't shake the images of the dead from his mind. Clearly the intense sketches of the temblement de terre would be permanently rooted in his mind.

He looked into a small mirror. Jean Carmelo couldn't believe what he saw. His left eyelid began to violently twitch.

Hours later, they touched down gently on the runway outside Orlando International Airport. Tired and physically beaten, everyone exited the aircraft in a long, single-file line of silence. Airport personnel guided them inside the airport for an ID and passport verification check. From there, members of the Red Cross greeted them with warm smiles and comforting words. They escorted the survivors into a large, brightly lit room with tables, soft lounge chairs, and help stations. They were offered snacks, bottled water, toiletries, phone access, and assistance with arranging hotel stays or flights to their next destinations.

Eating multiple bags of barbeque chips didn't feel right, but they were an immediate way to try to quiet his discontent. He sat in one of the chairs and laid his head back while waiting for his turn to be helped. He saw the televisions on the wall, but the pictures were a blur and the sounds couldn't get past the cloud of concern circling his brain.

An older man who had been on the plane walked over, put his bags down, and sat a short distance away. His body language suggested he had a load of questions—personal questions Jean Carmelo probably didn't want to answer. After a few minutes of small talk, the older man obviously realized that Jean Carmelo's limited Kreyol would not allow for deeper conversation. He was called off to conduct his personal business with one of the counselors, leaving Carmelo to return to his mental zone.

Jean Carmelo arranged a flight to Miami that would leave the next afternoon. From there, a connecting flight would take him to New York. After another fifteen-minute wait, a shuttle bus arrived to take him to the hotel located on the airport grounds. His hotel room was on the twelfth floor. It was simple but elegant, and he walked straight to the opposite end of the room. He pulled back the dark drapes to reveal the sliding glass doors and a beautiful view of the city.

That night, Jean Carmelo's firm bed was comfortable, but his sleep was uneasy. The tightly tucked bedspreads were the only thing that kept him from tossing and turning. There was silence in the room, but constant noise inside his head. The stench of man no longer surrounded his nose, but his canals remained congested as if the slightest possibility of inhaling something unsatisfactory kept him from breathing too deeply.

He woke up with the sun and turned on the television. For the first time, he got to see the images and hear the commentary from the American media. The more he watched reporters describe the tragedy he'd just left, the more he second-guessed whether or not he should have left. Rose had brought extra insulin, but how long would it last? Jules wouldn't be able to defend himself in another emergency. Jean Carmelo was in a nice hotel while the two people he'd known his whole life were trying to survive the most unpredictable existence. He didn't know what to do. The images on the television only made his mind numb. He took clippers from his bag and walked to the bathroom to shave. The buzzing head and face massage allowed him to relax for a few minutes and concentrate on a task he could complete. He tried to think of other small goals to set and accomplish.

It had been a while since he last ate, so he decided to stop by the restaurants he'd seen on the way to the hotel. The quarter-mile walk to get there was what he needed to help clear his thoughts. Green grass, measured sidewalks, ponds, ducks, and clean air stood out like never before. They had always been there as some of the aspects of life he took for granted.

It wasn't until he sat down to order that he realized he wasn't hungry. The greasy fried food cooking in the kitchen smelled familiar. He was drawn to it as a way to integrate back into society. He felt as though he had been away for a long time. He ordered what he always got when dining at diners: a feta cheese and spinach omelet with a glass of water and lemon.

He overheard a group of two women and two men in the booth behind him. They had just finished eating and were settling their bill while talking about how tragic the rising death tolls were in Haiti. They wished they could help those in need. They sounded as though they genuinely wanted to help, so Jean Carmelo turned around and introduced himself.

"I just came from over there," he said.

"From Haiti?" said one of the women in disbelief.

"Yes, I flew back here last night."

"My God! Were you in the actual earthquake? I hope you don't mind me asking," she added as almost an afterthought.

"I was...I was in the heart of Port-au-Prince."

"Hi. My name is Jane. I don't mean to be rude, but I'm a reporter for a local paper. Would you mind if I interviewed you on camera?" she said, pointing at a mid-sized professional video camera on the floor by one of the men.

"You should spread the word that the people there need help real bad. I would like to remain off camera though."

She nodded. "Yes, that's the least we can do. We really want to help."

He exchanged information with the group before they left.

Later that night, he prepared to board a plane the next morning that would connect at Miami International Airport before flying to JFK.

Back in New York, Augustin was waiting to embrace Jean Carmelo at the train station. They rode home together and caught up.

The next day, Jean Carmelo attempted to cope with the change in environment. New York was where he'd been comfortable just a few weeks ago, but he felt as though he'd been gone for years. Sitting behind the wheel of his car and showing restraint at a traffic light felt strange. Driving the 40-mph speed limit felt way too slow. He saw more traffic signals and stop signs in half a mile than he had seen in all of Port-au-Prince. His peripheral view shrank. All he did was stare straight ahead and think. He thought about everything but couldn't focus on anything.

He stopped at a convenience store to pick up a phone card to call Haiti. He tried to connect with the phone number his mother had given him. After following the instructions on the back of the card, he heard a slow ringing over crackling static.

"Halo?" a woman on the line answered.

"Oui, halo?"

"Halo?

"Oui, halo?"

Jean Carmelo remembered as a kid, he'd always looked at his mom funny when she called family members long-distance. She practically screamed into the phone and repeated things over and over. Phone communication between the two countries had always been poor. Jean Carmelo heard the echo of his voice, but the woman on the other end couldn't hear him. After numerous unsuccessful attempts to be heard he hung up and tried the same number again.

"Halo?" the same woman answered.

"Eske mwen ka pab parle avec Rose?" *Can I speak with Rose?* he said. It wasn't grammatically correct, but she would understand.

"C'est Carmelo?"

"Oui, Lauren, kijan ou ye?" *How are you?* he said, still hearing his own voice a half-second after each word he spoke.

"Mwen se oke. Manman ou se nan chanm nan pwochen an. Kite m 'jwenn li pou ou." *I'm okay. Your mother is in the next room. Let me get her for you.*

"Okay." He let loose a sigh of relief. Now he just had to make sure he got his message across loud and clear.

"Carmelo?" his mother said.

"Yes, I'm here in New York. I'm fine."

"I'm so happy you made it home. Did you see Augustin?"

"Yes, he's doing well," he said, speaking over his own echo.

Rose didn't seem to hear an echo on her side, so they were talking over each other. "Did you go to work?"

"Ma, forget about that. You have to go to the airport right away! American citizens with passports are allowed to leave the country."

"That's what I heard people saying. So I don't need to bring the plane tickets?"

"No, I took a giant military plane to get here. Just go to the airport. You'll be safer there. Don't worry about the day or time on your original plane ticket."

"Okay. I'll stay here until the end of the week. Emmanuel's eye is giving him problems, and I have to make sure he sees a doctor."

Jean Carmelo sighed. "It's been hard for me to sleep. How's Dad?"

"He's still not moving well, but we'll manage. We miss you too. Don't worry. God is watching over us."

"I'm gonna call you every day until you return. Is this the best number to reach you?"

"Yes. I'll do my best to be available at this number."

"I love you, Mom."

"Thank you, son. I love you too."

A week later, Rose and Jules flew safely into Miami. Shortly after, they received word that all was not well. Emmanuel had passed away. He lost his battle to the numerous health issues he had been suffering from quietly over the years. The increased stress in Haiti only added on to his problems. Not long after, Rose flew back to prepare the funeral arrangements for her brother.

The 2010 earthquake in Haiti represented one of the most devastating events in modern history. Killing over 300,000 people, affecting more than 3 million people, and causing an estimated $13 billion in damages, its impact was profound. Thirty seconds of horror created wounds that will take generations to heal. It tested Jean Carmelo, Rose, and Jules like they'd never been tried before, forcing them to confront loss and rebuild from ruins, both physical and emotional. Despite the odds that were stacked against them, they accomplished their planned mission, their resilience mirroring that of Haiti itself.

The earthquake was one in a long line of social, political, and natural disasters that have plagued the nation since its revolutionary birth. The hearts of the people remain unquestionable, their spirits forged in the same fire that created the world's first free Black republic, but the country's collective consciousness has yet to reach the same page.

The violence in Port-au-Prince, which stems from a lack of jobs and poverty remains entrenched. Political corruption continues, keeping valuable resources from the poor, a pattern that began with France's extortion of billions in "reparations" and continues with modern exploitation. Billions of aid dollars were raised by donor countries and financial institutions across the globe following the earthquake, promising reconstruction and renewal. Yet these funds have largely failed to reach the millions of Haitians in need, lost in a labyrinth of international bureaucracy, mismanagement, and self-serving interests.

Meanwhile, children and young adults search for scarce opportunities in a landscape where hope itself becomes an act of rebellion. The everyday struggle to rebuild the damaged infrastructure and progress continues, not just from the earthquake but from centuries of external interference and internal division. Through it all, the Haitian people endure, carrying forward the revolutionary spirit of their ancestors, waiting for the day when their nation's extraordinary resilience will finally be matched by extraordinary justice.

What to Do When an Earthquake Strikes?

In the event of an earthquake, taking immediate and appropriate action is crucial for your safety. While each earthquake presents unique challenges, experts widely recommend a straightforward strategy known as Drop, Cover, and Hold On.

The ground's movement during an earthquake can be erratic and forceful, ranging from sharp jolts to a rolling motion akin to a ship at sea. To avoid being knocked off your feet, the first step is to Drop to your hands and knees. If you use a wheelchair, ensure you lock the wheels to maintain stability.

Next, Cover your head and neck – vital areas vulnerable to injury – with your arms. If a sturdy table or desk is within reach, crawl underneath it for further protection. If such shelter isn't immediately available, move against an interior wall, away from windows and exterior walls. (It's important to note that seeking refuge in a doorway is no longer considered a safe practice.)

Finally, Hold On. If you are under a table or desk, grip one of its legs firmly and stay in place until the shaking ceases. If you are against an interior wall, protect your head and neck with your arms and remain there.

If Indoors: Resist the natural urge to run outside during the shaking. The exterior of buildings can be hazardous due to falling debris, such as glass and building materials. You also risk being knocked down in the violent shaking.

If Outdoors: If you find yourself outside when an earthquake begins, stay outdoors. Try to move to an open area away from buildings, streetlights, power lines, and trees that could potentially fall.

Important Considerations: While the "Drop, Cover, and Hold On" advice is generally applicable, there is a notable exception. According to the Earthquake Country Alliance, if you are on the ground floor of a building constructed with minimal engineering oversight, such as mud-brick structures, you should consider moving outside during the shaking if it is safe to do so.

After the Shaking Stops: The dangers do not end when the ground stops shaking. Be aware of potential hazards such as leaking gas lines, downed electrical wires, and the risk of fire. If you are in a coastal area, be particularly vigilant for tsunami warnings.

Furthermore, aftershocks, smaller earthquakes that follow the main shock, are common and can cause additional damage or collapses. If you are in a heavily damaged building and it is safe to evacuate, do so, and if possible, take essential documents and medications with you, as re-entry may not be possible.

By understanding these guidelines and remaining calm, you can significantly increase your safety during and after an earthquake.

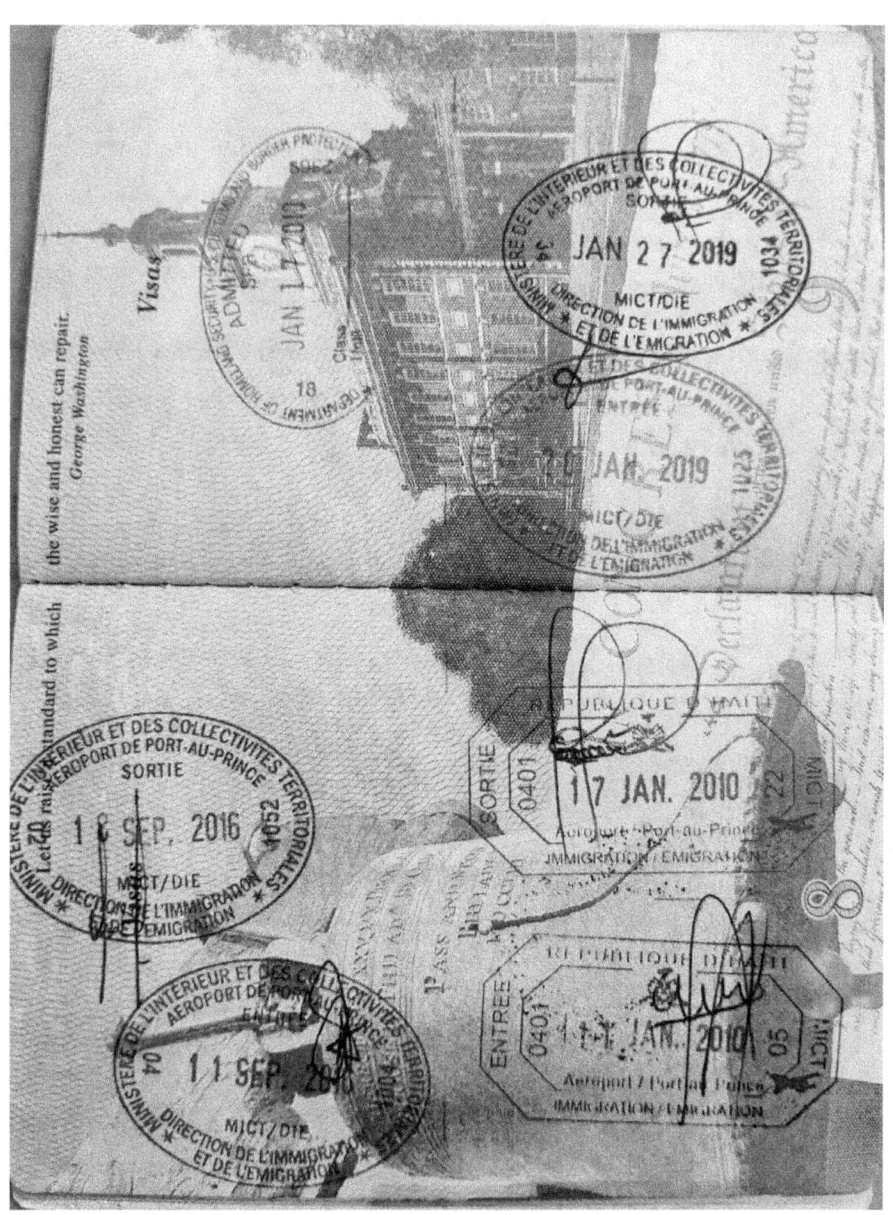

ACKNOWLEDGMENTS

The journey of writing this book has undoubtedly been the most demanding intellectual undertaking I have ever embraced. Its realization is owed to the support and contributions of numerous individuals, far too many to name exhaustively here.

I must first express my profound gratitude for the dedicated teachers who have enriched my intellectual life. Their passion for education and the vibrant energy they brought to the learning process were foundational to my development.

A special acknowledgment is due to Drew Spence. Your unwavering patience throughout the countless revisions of this work was indispensable. Our many discussions and thoughtful debates played a crucial role in refining its strengths and enhancing its overall quality.

Cassie Cox, thank you for your prompt and meticulous editing of my debut book. Your keen eye and swift responses were invaluable.

Charles Loiseau, your steadfast support has been a constant source of encouragement. Your willingness to read and reread my drafts meant the world to me.

Rose Coogan, your genuine spirit and insightful perspective have been a golden resource. Your dedicated work ethic as a fellow writer is truly inspiring.

Doris Bodet, thank you for your reliable and nuanced work as one of my key translators. Your linguistic expertise was essential.

Rose Nesmy Saint-Louis, your positive words offered a much-needed beacon of light at the outset of this endeavor. Your encouragement was deeply appreciated.

Jeff Carey, your refreshing honesty and direct feedback were invaluable. Thank you for your candid insights.

I also wish to acknowledge the Florida International University professor who taught my freshman composition class in 1992. While your name escapes me now, I vividly recall the day you called me to the front of the classroom. Expecting news of a poor grade, I was instead met with a question that would resonate for years to come: "Have you ever considered becoming a writer?" Though I didn't fully grasp the significance of that moment then, it undeniably became a pivotal turning point in my life's trajectory.

Finally, I extend my sincere gratitude to Dr. Tracy Fitzsimmons and the dedicated students of Shenandoah University for their commendable work with College Catherine Flon in Carrefour, Haiti. Your commitment to education and community building is truly inspiring. Thank you also to the Wells Mountain Initiative for providing the invaluable opportunities to return to Haiti after the devastating earthquake and contribute to the construction of vital community centers in partnership with the YMCA d'Haiti. Your support has been instrumental in fostering hope and rebuilding lives.

ABOUT THE AUTHOR

Will, CEO of True Iron Will, is a dedicated healthspan optimization strategist. Recognizing the interconnectedness of well-being, he founded True Iron Will, a holistic lifestyle company that provides a unique and impactful approach to personal transformation. His work seamlessly blends hands-on wellness coaching with transformative literary guidance, enabling clients to unlock sustainable health and vitality throughout their lives.

Thank you for reading. If you found this book to be of any value, I would be grateful if you could spread the good word and refer it to someone who could appreciate it.

Best of health,

Will

TrueIronWill.com

www.ingramcontent.com/pod-product-compliance
Lightning Source LLC
Chambersburg PA
CBHW071239130626
46556CB00003B/1079